P9-EDC-256

SouthernLiving

Oxmoor House®

Southern Living® Basic Wiring was adapted from a book by the same title published by Sunset Books.

Consulting Editor: Don Vandervort
Editorial coordinator: Vicki Weathers

Staff for this book:
Senior Editor: Elizabeth Cameron
Senior Art Director: Francine Lemieux
Art Director: Solange Laberge
Designers: François Daxhelet, Hélène Dion,
   Jean-Guy Doiron, François Longpré
Picture Editor: Christopher Jackson
Contributing Illustrators: Michel Blais, Jacques Perrault
Production Manager: Michelle Turbide
System Coordinators: Eric Beaulieu, Jean-Luc Roy
Photographers: Robert Chartier, Christian Levesque
Proofreader: Jane Pavanel
Indexer: Christine M. Jacobs
Administrator: Natalie Watanabe
Other Staff: Chantal Bilodeau, Normand Boudreault,
   Lorraine Doré, Michel Giguère, Heather Mills,
   Adam van Sertima

Cover: Design by James Boone and Vasken Guiragossian.
Photography by Noel Barnhurst. Photo styling by
Mary Ann Cleary.

Our appreciation to the staff of *Southern Living* magazine for their contributions to this book.

Acknowledgments
Thanks to the following:
AT&T Corp., Parsippany, NJ
René Bertrand, Blainville, Que.
Centre Do-It D'Agostino, Montreal, Que.
Hydro-Québec, Montreal, Que.
Kenneth Larsen, C. Howard Simpkin Ltd., Montreal, Que.
National Fire Protection Association, Quincy, MA
Edward Devereux Sheffe, New York, NY
3M Canada Inc., London, Ont.
Walter Tomalty Enterprises Ltd., Montreal, Que.
Underwriters' Laboratories, Melville, NY

First printing January 1999
Copyright © 1999 by Oxmoor House, Inc.
Book Division of Southern Progress Corporation
P.O. Box 2463, Birmingham, Alabama 35201
Pages 78 to 89 copyright © 1996 AT&T Corp.

Southern Living® is a federally registered trademark of
Southern Living, Inc.

ISBN 0-376-09054-5
Library of Congress Catalog Card Number: 98-87004
Printed in the United States

TOOLS OF THE TRADE

You can handle most electrical repairs in the home with the specialized tools shown below. Many of these tools, such as diagonal-cutting pliers, lineman's pliers, and wire strippers make it easier and safer to prepare wire ends and to make sound wire connections at lamp sockets, switches, receptacles, and other electrical devices. The versatile multipurpose tool strips insula-

tion from wires, and its blades slice through wire. The tool also can be used to attach crimp connectors to wire ends. A fish tape is an indispensable addition to your toolkit if you are planning to route wire behind existing walls, ceilings, and flooring. Always use a neon tester to confirm that power to the circuit is off before beginning any electrical work.

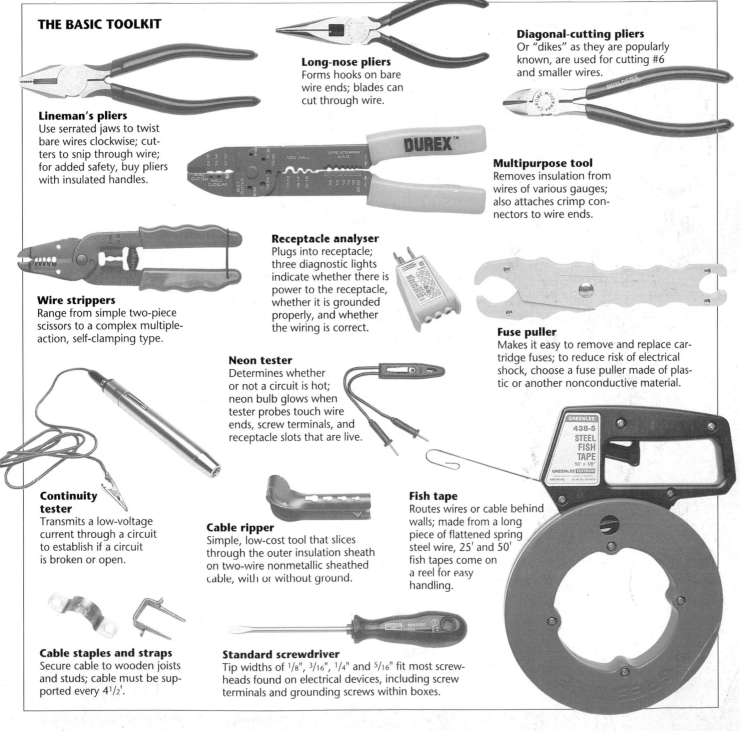

THE BASIC TOOLKIT

Long-nose pliers
Forms hooks on bare wire ends; blades can cut through wire.

Diagonal-cutting pliers
Or "dikes" as they are popularly known, are used for cutting #6 and smaller wires.

Lineman's pliers
Use serrated jaws to twist bare wires clockwise; cutters to snip through wire; for added safety, buy pliers with insulated handles.

Multipurpose tool
Removes insulation from wires of various gauges; also attaches crimp connectors to wire ends.

Wire strippers
Range from simple two-piece scissors to a complex multiple-action, self-clamping type.

Receptacle analyser
Plugs into receptacle; three diagnostic lights indicate whether there is power to the receptacle, whether it is grounded properly, and whether the wiring is correct.

Fuse puller
Makes it easy to remove and replace cartridge fuses; to reduce risk of electrical shock, choose a fuse puller made of plastic or another nonconductive material.

Neon tester
Determines whether or not a circuit is hot; neon bulb glows when tester probes touch wire ends, screw terminals, and receptacle slots that are live.

Continuity tester
Transmits a low-voltage current through a circuit to establish if a circuit is broken or open.

Cable ripper
Simple, low-cost tool that slices through the outer insulation sheath on two-wire nonmetallic sheathed cable, with or without ground.

Fish tape
Routes wires or cable behind walls; made from a long piece of flattened spring steel wire, 25' and 50' fish tapes come on a reel for easy handling.

Cable staples and straps
Secure cable to wooden joists and studs; cable must be supported every 4 1/2'.

Standard screwdriver
Tip widths of 1/8", 3/16", 1/4" and 5/16" fit most screwheads found on electrical devices, including screw terminals and grounding screws within boxes.

TYPES OF CABLES AND WIRES

A cable consists of two or more wires contained in the same protective outer sheathing. A single conductor is an individual wire, usually sheathed with an insulating material. We say "usually" because a grounding wire may be bare, particularly when it is contained within a cable.

American Wire Gauge (AWG) numbers are assigned to electrical wires to indicate their diameter. The numbers refer to the metal conductor only, and do not include the insulation. These numbers appear on the cable sheathing, as well as on the individual wires protected within the sheathing.

Cable is identified by the size and number of conductors it contains. For example, a cable with two #14 wires (one white and one black) and a grounding wire (green or bare) is called a "14-2 with ground." Nonmetallic sheathed cable is used in most residential wiring. Nonmetallic sheathed cable comes in types: NM (nonmetallic) and UF (underground feeder). Type AC metal-clad cable and nonflexible and flexible conduit, although more difficult and expensive to install than NM cable, are other options for indoor wiring projects; if your local code requires conduit, it's best to consult a professional.

Single conductors (individual wires) are shielded from one another by material that does not carry current—color-coded thermoplastic. White or gray insulation indicates neutral wires, green is used for grounding wires, and all other colors (red, black, blue, etc.) are used to identify hot wires.

Although copper is the best and most commonly used metal for conductors, aluminum and copper-clad aluminum are also used. Because aluminum is not as efficient a conductor as copper, aluminum or copper-clad aluminum wire must be larger than a copper wire in order to conduct the same amount of electricity.

Table II and Table III, on the facing page, list the conductor currents permitted by the *National Electrical Code® (NEC)®*. These tables apply when there are no more than three current-carrying conductors in a cable or enclosure.

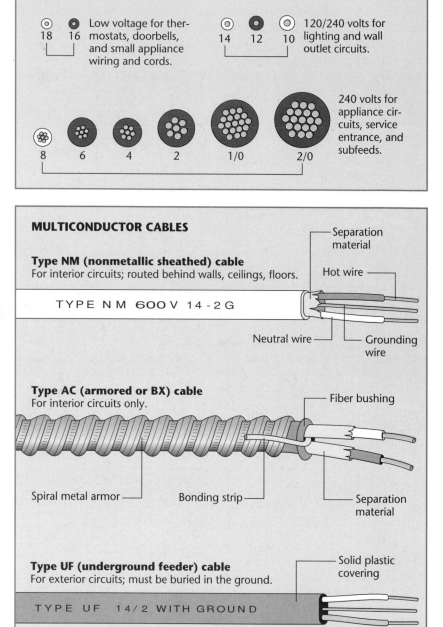

CROSS SECTIONS OF COPPER CONDUCTORS

18 16 Low voltage for thermostats, doorbells, and small appliance wiring and cords.

14 12 10 120/240 volts for lighting and wall outlet circuits.

8 6 4 2 1/0 2/0

240 volts for appliance circuits, service entrance, and subfeeds.

MULTICONDUCTOR CABLES

Type NM (nonmetallic sheathed) cable
For interior circuits; routed behind walls, ceilings, floors.

TYPE NM 600V 14-2G

Separation material — Hot wire — Neutral wire — Grounding wire

Type AC (armored or BX) cable
For interior circuits only.

Fiber bushing — Spiral metal armor — Bonding strip — Separation material

Type UF (underground feeder) cable
For exterior circuits; must be buried in the ground.

TYPE UF 14/2 WITH GROUND

Solid plastic covering

Neutral wires twisted together to make single conductor

Type SE (service entrance) cable
Brings electricity to the service panel.

6 AWG TYPE SE

TABLE I THREE COMMON THERMOPLASTIC-INSULATED CONDUCTORS

Type	Max. operating temperature	Application
TW	60 C, 140 F	Dry and wet locations
THW	75 C, 167 F	Dry and wet locations
THWN	75 C, 167 F	Dry and wet locations

TABLE II ALLOWABLE AMPACITY OF INSULATED COPPER CONDUCTORS

Wire size	Insulation type	Ampacity
14	TW, THW, THWN	15
12	TW, THW, THWN	20
10	TW, THW, THWN	30
8	TW	40
8	THW, THWN	50
6	TW	55
6	THW, THWN	65
4	TW	70
4	THW*, THWN*	85
2	TW	95
2	THW*, THWN*	115
1	THW*, THWN*	130
2/0	THW*, THWN*	175

*Exception—the following ampacities apply when used as service entrance conductors and service laterals and feeders that carry the total load to dwelling units, 120/240-volt 3-wire single phase only.

4	THW, THWN	100
2	THW, THWN	125
1	THW, THWN	150
2/0	THW, THWN	200

TABLE III ALLOWABLE AMPACITY OF INSULATED ALUMINUM AND COPPER-CLAD ALUMINUM CONDUCTORS

Wire size	Insulation type	Ampacity
12	TW, THW, THWN	15
10	TW, THW, THWN	25
8	TW	30
8	THW, THWN	40
6	TW	40
6	THW, THWN	50
4	TW	55
4	THW, THWN	65
2	TW	75
2	THW*, THWN*	90
1/0	TW	100
1/0	THW*, THWN*	120
2/0	THW, THWN	135
4/0	THW*, THWN*	180

*Exception—the following ampacities apply when used as service entrance conductors and service laterals and feeders that carry the total load to dwelling units, 120/240-volt 3-wire single phase only.

2	THW, THWN	100
1/0	THW, THWN	120
4/0	THW, THWN	200

Reprinted with permission from NFPA 70-1993, the National Electrical Code®, Copyright© 1993, National Fire Protection Association, Quincy, MA 02269. This reprinted material is not the complete and official position of the National Fire Protection Association on the referenced subject, which is represented only by the standard in its entirety.

TABLE IV NUMBER OF CONDUCTORS PER BOX

Type of box	Size	Number of conductors			
		#14	#12	#10	#8
Octagonal	4"x1¼"	6	5	5	4
	4"x1½"	7	6	6	5
	4"x2⅛"	10	9	8	7
Square	4"x1¼"	9	8	7	6
	4"x1½"	10	9	8	7
	4"x2⅛"	15	13	12	10
	4¹¹/₁₆"x1¼"	12	11	10	8
	4¹¹/₁₆"x1½"	14	13	11	9
Switch	3"x2"x2¼"	5	4	4	3
	3"x2"x2½"	6	5	5	4
	3"x2"x2¾"	7	6	5	4
	3"x2"x3½"	9	8	7	6

*Count all grounding wires as one conductor.
Count each hickey, cable clamp, fixture stud, receptacle, and switch as one conductor.
Count each wire entering and leaving box without splice as one conductor.
Pigtails are not counted at all.

TESTING DEVICES

Two basic diagnostic tools are available to help in electrical work. The first is a neon tester; the second is a continuity tester.

Neon tester: Use a neon tester to confirm that the circuit is dead before you touch bare wire ends. Be careful using the neon tester: you may be near live wires. Always hold the probes by their insulation and use the probes carefully. A carelessly placed probe can cause a short circuit if it accidentally touches both a hot and a grounded object at the same time.

Continuity tester: A battery-powered continuity tester sends a low-voltage current through a circuit to determine if the electrical path is undamaged. There are several different kinds of continuity testers. One type contains a battery and light; another uses a battery and a buzzer or bell. Use either form of continuity tester to tell whether a circuit is open or broken, or whether a short circuit exists. Before you use a continuity tester, make very sure the power is off—at the service panel, either turn off the breaker or pull the fuse *(page 21)*.

Using a neon tester

Checking to confirm that a circuit is dead
Grasping the tester leads only by their insulated handles, touch one probe to a hot wire or terminal and the other probe to a neutral wire or terminal, to the equipment grounding conductor, or to the grounded metal box. If the tester lights, the circuit is hot; if it does not light, you have killed power to the right circuit.

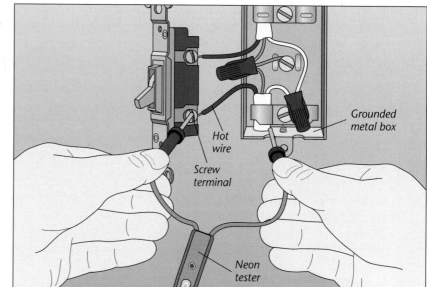

Hot wire

Screw terminal

Grounded metal box

Neon tester

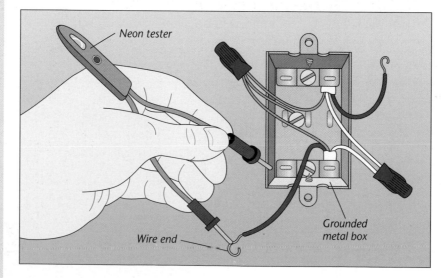

Neon tester

Wire end

Grounded metal box

Finding a hot wire
To determine which is the hot wire of a two-wire circuit with ground, touch one probe to the grounding wire or metal box and touch the other probe to the other wires, one at a time. The tester lights when the second probe touches the hot wire.

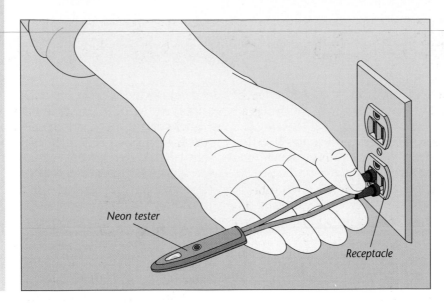

Neon tester

Receptacle

When you've just unplugged a lamp or appliance because it doesn't work, the neon tester can tell you whether the appliance is at fault or the circuit is dead. Insert the tester probes into the slots of a receptacle; if the tester lights up, the circuit is receiving power.

Using a continuity tester

Testing electrical devices

A battery-powered tester sends a small electrical current through a device, such as a cartridge fuse, switch, socket, or wire, to determine if its path is undamaged. If the tester lights (or buzzes), the device is sound. To test a cartridge fuse, first remove the fuse from the fuse block. Touch the tester probes to each end of the fuse. If the fuse is good, the tester will light (or buzz).

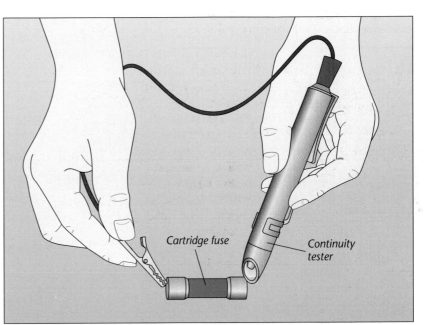

Cartridge fuse

Continuity tester

MAKING A CONTINUITY TESTER

You'll need a doorbell, a 6-volt dry cell battery, and two lengths of wire. Use a short length of wire to connect one battery terminal to a terminal on the back of the doorbell. Next, connect another 2-foot-long wire to the other terminal on the back of the doorbell. Check the tester by touching the free wire end to the free battery terminal momentarily. The doorbell should ring.

Short wire

Doorbell

2-foot-long wire

6-volt battery

WORKING WITH CABLE AND WIRE

Cable consists of insulated and bare wires bundled together and wrapped in an outer sheath of insulation. Before connecting a cable to a device or joining it to another cable, cut open and remove the outer sheath, cut away all separation materials, and strip the insulation from the ends of the individual conductors.

To lay open cable, such as two-wire NM (with or without ground), use a cable ripper or knife. If you're using round, three-wire cable—as when you're wiring three-way switches—use a pocket knife, linoleum knife, or utility knife so you can follow the rotation of the wires without cutting into their insulation.

Do not cut open cable while it rests on your knee or thigh. Use a flat board or wall surface. Also, don't cut toward your body—always cut away from it.

Once you've exposed the wires, cutting off the outer sheath and any separation materials, you are ready to strip the insulation off the ends of the wires.

How to rip cable

TOOLKIT
• Cable ripper
• Diagonal-cutting pliers

1 ▶ Slicing through the sheath
To remove the outer insulation from a cable, slide a cable ripper up the cable to the top of box. Press the handles of the cable ripper together and pull toward the end of cable. This will score the outer sheath. Bend the cable back to crack the score and then peel open the outer sheath of insulation.

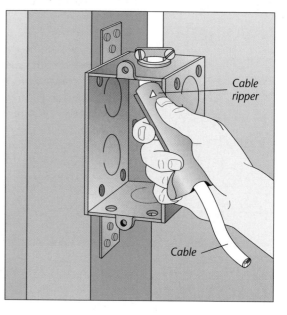

Cable ripper

Cable

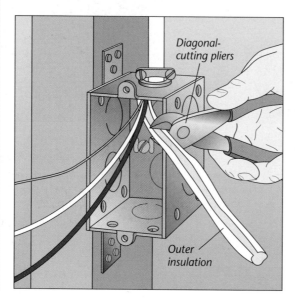

Diagonal-cutting pliers

Outer insulation

◀ 2 Cutting off the insulation
Separate the wires from the insulation. Using a pair of diagonal-cutting pliers, cut off the opened outer sheath of insulation and all separation materials.

MAKING WIRE CONNECTIONS

Use a wire stripper to peel off the outer insulation from a wire. Be careful not to nick the wire when you are stripping off its insulation. A nicked wire will break easily, especially since the nick is usually right where you bend the wire to form a loop for a connection to a screw terminal. If you do nick a wire, snip off the damaged wire end and begin again.

Solid wires from #14 to #10 are easily stripped using a wire stripper or the graduated wire stripper jaws on a multipurpose tool. The illustrations opposite show how to use the stripper. After you've practiced the movement several times it will become quite easy. To strip larger wires—#8 to #4/0—use a pocket knife to take off the insulation as if you were sharpening a pencil. Cut away from your body.

Joining wires: Wires are joined together (spliced) with solderless, mechanical connectors. These connectors are of two basic types: wire nuts and compression sleeves. Note: If you must splice aluminum wire to copper wire, use a special two-compartment connector.

Wire nuts: Wire nuts come in about four sizes to accommodate various wire combinations. They cannot be used for wires larger than #6. Each manufacturer has its own color code to distinguish the various sizes. For example, in one brand a red wire nut can be used to splice four #12 wires or five #14 wires. Once you know how many wires of what size you'll be splicing, make sure you get the proper wire nut sizes. The packaging will tell you what wires the various sizes of wire nuts will take.

Compression sleeves: You can use the special jaws on a wire stripper or multipurpose tool to attach these connectors; there is also a special two- or four-jawed crimping tool for the same purpose. Once you've stripped two or more wires and twisted them together, slide the metal sleeve over the wires, and use the tool to press the sleeve onto them. Make sure that you use enough pressure to shape the metal into tight contact. An insulating cap then fits over the connection, as shown on page 12.

Some jurisdictions require use of compression sleeves for grounding wires because they provide a more permanent bond than wire nuts. If you are in doubt about your local regulations, contact your municipal building department. When used to connect grounding wires, a compression sleeve need not be covered with an insulating cap.

How to strip and secure wire

TOOLKIT
• Wire stripper
• Long-nose pliers

1 ▶ Removing the insulation
Using a wire stripper, insert the wire into the matching slot, or set the adjustment screw for the gauge of wire. Holding the wire firmly in your hand with your thumb extended toward the end of the wire, position the stripper on the wire at an angle and press the handles together. Rock the stripper back and forth until the insulation is severed and can be pulled off the wire.

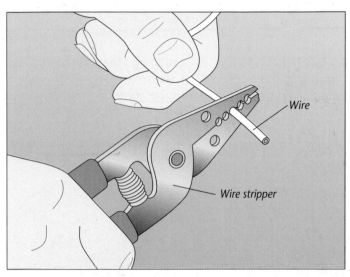

Wire

Wire stripper

◀ 2 Forming a hook
To make wire-to-screw-terminal connections, strip about 1/2" to 3/4" of insulation off the wire end. Using long-nose pliers, form a two-third to three-quarter loop in the bare wire. Starting near the insulation, bend the wire at a right angle and make progressive bends , moving the pliers toward the wire end until a loop is formed.

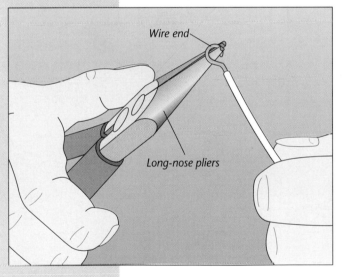

Wire end

Long-nose pliers

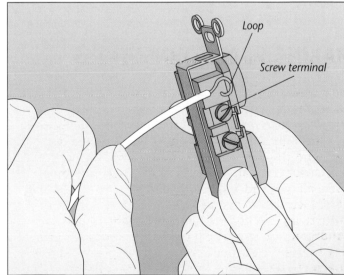

Loop

Screw terminal

3 ▶ Securing a terminal connection
Hook the wire clockwise around the screw terminal. As you tighten the screw, the loop on the wire will close. If you hook the wire backward (counterclockwise), tightening the screw will tend to open the loop.

MAKING SOUND CONNECTIONS

Always strip your wires so that a minimum (no more than ¹/₁₆ inch) of bare wire extends out beyond the screw head, or for that matter, beyond any connector. On the other hand, don't let the insulation extend into the clamped area. If necessary, unscrew the connection and start again.

Don't try to place more than a single wire under a screw terminal, because the terminals are made for only one wire. If you need to join several wires at a single screw terminal, use a pigtail splice.

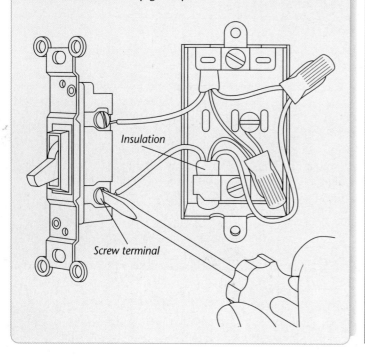

Insulation

Screw terminal

MAKING A PIGTAIL SPLICE

This arrangement is nothing more than three or more wires spliced together. One of the wires (the pigtail) connects to a terminal on an electrical device such as a switch or receptacle. The pigtail wire, usually 6 inches long, must match the gauge of the other wires in the splice. A wire nut or a compression sleeve is used to secure the splice. Electrician's tape should never be used in place of a wire nut. Tape is useful for emergency insulation repairs, but it's not a substitute for a good mechanical splice.

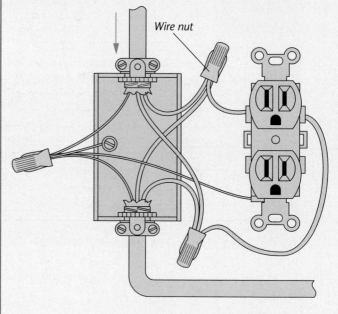

Wire nut

How to put on a wire nut or a compression sleeve

TOOLKIT

For wire nut:
• Wire strippers
• Diagonal-cutting pliers (optional)

For compression sleeve:
• Wire strippers
• Diagonal-cutting pliers
• Multipurpose tool

Screwing on a wire nut

Strip off about 1" of insulation from the ends of the wires you're going to join. It is not necessary to twist the wires together before using a wire nut; the action of screwing on the wire nut twists them together. Holding the wires parallel, screw the wire nut on clockwise until it is tight and no bare wire is exposed *(right)*.

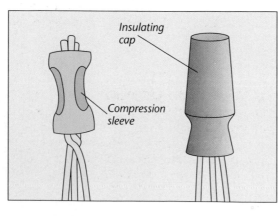

Insulating cap

Compression sleeve

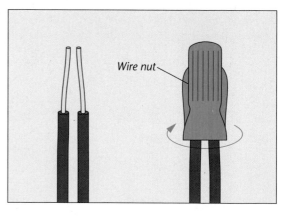

Wire nut

Putting on a compression sleeve

Twist the wire ends clockwise at least one and one-half turns. Snip ³/₈" to ¹/₂" off the twisted ends so that they are even. Slip a compression sleeve onto the wire ends, and crimp the sleeve using a multi-purpose tool. Put on an insulating cap.

Making connections with stranded wire

TOOLKIT

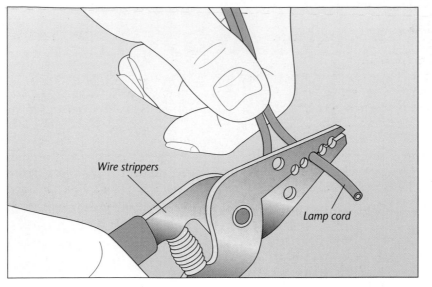

Wire strippers

Lamp cord

1 Removing the insulation
Stranded wire commonly is found in lamp cord. To make a wire connection using stranded wire, begin by stripping about ³/₄" of insulation from the wire end using wire strippers *(left)*.

2 Preparing the wire ends
Twist the exposed strands in each wire together tightly in a clockwise direction using your thumb and forefinger *(right)*. To attach the wire to a screw terminal, shape the twisted strands into a loop and hook it around a screw terminal in a clockwise direction. Tighten the screw, making sure that no stray wire ends are exposed.

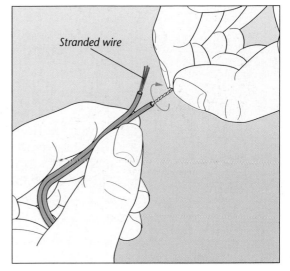

Stranded wire

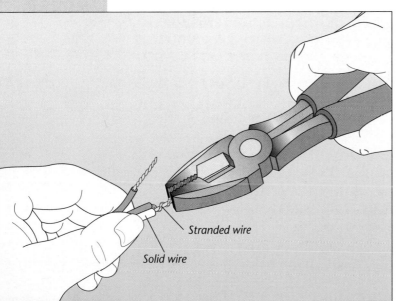

Stranded wire

Solid wire

3 Attaching stranded wire to solid wire
To attach a stranded wire to a solid wire, first strip about ³/₄" of insulation from both wire ends, twisting the stranded wire end tightly in a clockwise direction. Position the two wire ends so that they are parallel to each other and wrap the stranded wire around the solid wire in a spiral fashion. To secure the splice, fold the exposed wire ends using lineman's pliers and screw on a wire nut.

PLAY IT SAFE

REMOVING INSULATION FROM STRANDED WIRE
When removing the outer insulation from lamp cord, be careful not to break any strands of the wire. Never use a utility knife to remove the insulation; you risk cutting into some of the stranded wires; always use wire strippers. Once the insulation is removed, inspect the wire strands. If any of them are damaged, snip off the wire end and begin again.

AN INTRODUCTION TO THE BASICS

Electricity provides us with comfort and conveniences that we often take for granted unless something goes wrong. Fortunately for the do-it-yourselfer, electrical work is one of the easiest kinds of home maintenance and repair. It's simple, neat, and logical; it doesn't require a shop full of specialized tools; and there's considerable standardization in home electrical systems and related materials. But before you embark on any electrical wiring projects, it's important to understand a few things about electricity itself, electrical safety, and electrical codes.

This chapter provides you with a basic understanding of how electricity energizes your home, and how currents and circuits work. You'll learn how to work safely with electricity: how to shut off the main power supply at the service panel and electricity to a particular circuit, as well as how grounding protects your electrical system and guards against the possibility of electrical shock. You'll find out how to troubleshoot the source of a short circuit and what you can do if the lights go out *(page 22).* We'll help you evaluate your electrical assets by showing you how to map out your home's wiring plan, read your meter, and how to calculate your electrical usage.

To gain a better understanding of the way a home electrical system works, read on as we untangle the maze of wires, starting at the point where the utility company supplies your home with electricity.

Each circuit in your home is protected by a fuse or circuit breaker. If there is any problem with the circuit, the fuse will blow, or the circuit breaker will trip. Before beginning any electrical repair in this book, make sure you unscrew the fuse or trip the circuit breaker protecting the circuit you intend to work on.

HOW ELECTRICITY ENERGIZES YOUR HOME

Utility companies distribute power to individual households through overhead wires or underground cables. Today, most homes have three-wire service. That is, the utility company connects three lines to the service entrance equipment. With this arrangement, there are two "hot" conductors (wires), each supplying electricity at 120 volts, and one "neutral" conductor. During normal operation, this neutral wire is maintained at zero volts, or what is referred to as "ground potential."

Three-wire service provides both 120-volt and 240-volt capabilities. One hot conductor and the neutral combine to provide for 120-volt needs, such as light fixtures or wall receptacles (outlets). Both hot conductors combine with the neutral to provide 120/240 volts for large appliances, such as a range or clothes dryer.

Many older homes have a limited two-wire service. These homes have only one hot conductor at 120 volts and a neutral conductor. As a result, the electrical system may not be able to handle the higher voltage requirements of an electric range or dryer.

An explanation is in order about the designation of the voltage supplied by the utility company. As mentioned on page 16, voltage is electrical pressure. Furthermore, this pressure can fluctuate from roughly 115 volts to 125 volts, even within the same day. That is why you may see references elsewhere to household voltages other than 120. This book uses 120 as the voltage for each hot line from the utility company.

HOW DO THREE WIRES ENERGIZE YOUR HOME?

As shown in the illustration at right, electricity passes through a meter before it enters the service panel. Owned, installed, and serviced by the utility company, the meter is the final step in the installation of a complete wiring system. Once in place, the meter measures the electrical energy consumed in kilowatt-hours. ("Kilowatt-hours" refers to the rate of energy consumption in kilowatts multiplied by the time of usage in hours.)

The control center for an electrical system is the service panel, sometimes referred to as the fusebox, or panel box. This panel—a cabinet or box—usually houses the main disconnect (the main fuses or main circuit breaker), which shuts off power to the entire electrical system, and the fuses or circuit breakers that protect the individual circuits in the home.

Electricity runs from the utility company lines, through the meter, and into the service panel. Once inside the service panel it is divided into branch circuits that transmit power to the different parts of the house.

Typically, each cable contains three conductors. Two hot conductors (identified by red, black, or any other color except white, gray, or green insulation) go to the main disconnect. The neutral conductor (color-coded white or gray) goes directly to a device called the neutral bus bar.

There is one other important wire associated with your service panel—the grounding electrode conductor. The continuous conductor connects the neutral bus bar to the metal water supply pipe entering your home (a grounding jumper wire is used to bypass the water meter) and to a metal ground rod driven into the ground. This safety feature provides excess current with an uninterrupted metal pathway into the ground.

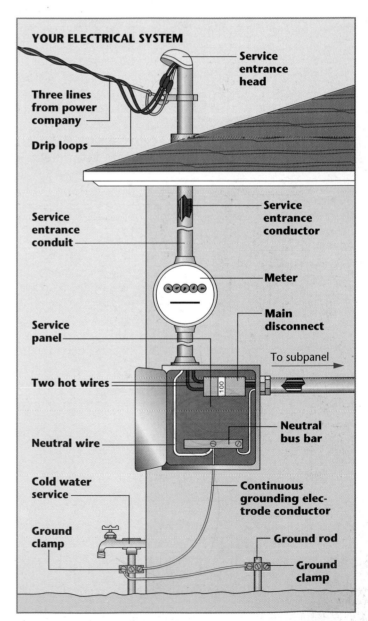

YOUR ELECTRICAL SYSTEM

- Three lines from power company
- Drip loops
- Service entrance head
- Service entrance conduit
- Service entrance conductor
- Meter
- Service panel
- Main disconnect
- To subpanel
- Two hot wires
- Neutral wire
- Neutral bus bar
- Cold water service
- Continuous grounding electrode conductor
- Ground clamp
- Ground rod
- Ground clamp

Learning to read your electric meter can help you keep close track of your energy consumption, check your electricity bill, or simply satisfy your curiosity about that silent, sleepless counter.

Most electric meters have four (older installations) or five (newer installations) dials with numbers and pointers. A quick look at one of these dials shows that their numbering alternates between clockwise and counterclockwise.

To take a reading of your meter, jot down the numbers indicated by the pointers, starting with the left dial. When the pointer is between two numbers, always read the smaller number. When the pointer appears to be directly on a number, check the next dial to the right. If the pointer of that dial is on zero or has passed zero, record the number indicated by the pointer of the first dial. If the pointer of the second dial has not yet reached zero, write down the next smaller number than the one indicated on the first dial.

In the example below, the pointer of the first (left-hand) dial is between 0 and 1, so the number to record is 0; in the second dial, the pointer is between 4 and 5, so write down the number 4. The pointer of the third dial is almost directly at 2, so look at the pointer of the fourth dial. It has passed 9 but not quite reached 0. For the third dial, then, 1 is the number to record; for the fourth dial the number is 9. And on the last dial, since the pointer is between 7 and 8; record the number 7. The reading is therefore 04197 kilowatt-hours.

If you want to figure out the number of kilowatt-hours consumed during a certain period of time, subtract the meter reading at the start of the period from the reading at the end. You can use this to check your utility bills.

CURRENTS AND CIRCUITS

Electricity is a current of very tiny particles (electrons) flowing through a wire. Associated with this flowing current are some terms you will work with often.

Watts: The energy supplied by the current (to light a light bulb, for instance), is expressed in watts.

Volts: The potential difference, or pressure, causing the current to flow is measured in volts.

Amperes: The amount of current that flows through the wire or device is measured in amperes (amps). For the purposes of this book, the relationship among these units is represented in this formula: volts x amperes = watts.

Path of least resistance: Another important characteristic of electric current is that it is choosy about the materials it flows through. It is partial to flowing in the path offering the least resistance.

Conductor: The general term "conductor" applies to anything that permits, or conducts, the flow of electricity rather than resisting it. Certain materials make better conductors than others. Copper, for example, is a good conductor; most wires are made of copper, although aluminum wiring is permitted. Wires come in different gauges, or sizes; the more current, or amperes, the larger the wire required. Rubber, on the other hand, is a very poor conductor, offering so much resistance that it's often used as an insulator to prevent any flow of electricity between conductors.

A glossary defining many other terms you might need to know is provided on page 95.

A glossary defining many other terms you might need to know is provided on page 95.

In order to flow, electric current must have a continuous path from start to finish—like a circle. The word "circuit" refers to the entire course an electric current travels, from the source of power through some device that uses electricity (such as a toaster) and back to its starting point, the source. Each circuit forms a continuous closed path that can be traced from its beginning in the service panel or subpanel through various receptacles or appliances and back to the service panel, or subpanel.

Cables deliver electricity from the service panel to the devices on the circuit. The black wire in each cable brings electrical current to the devices, and the white wire returns the current to the service panel. Cables also contain a bare copper wire. This wire protects the entire circuit by providing a backup pathway for electricity to return to the service panel.

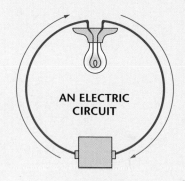

AN ELECTRIC CIRCUIT

Understanding basic electrical circuits

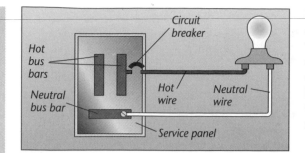

Circuit breaker

Hot bus bars

Neutral bus bar

Hot wire

Neutral wire

Service panel

Simple circuit

A circuit is a continuous closed path in which electricity flows from the source of voltage through a device, and back to the source. In the stylized example at left, the hot wire brings electricity to a light fixture and the neutral wire returns electricity to the service panel. The white wire is connected directly to the neutral bus bar in the service panel.

Parallel wiring

In most homes, several light fixtures operate on the same circuit by what is called "parallel wiring." With parallel wiring, the hot and neutral wires run continuously from one fixture box to another. Wires to the individual lights branch off from these continuous hot and neutral wires.

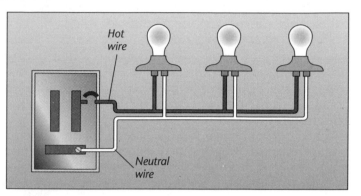

Hot wire

Neutral wire

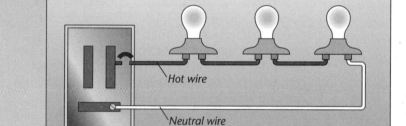

Hot wire

Neutral wire

Series wiring

Often contrasted to parallel wiring is series wiring. When light fixtures are wired in series, the hot wire passes through all of the lamps before joining the neutral wire that returns to the source. Series wiring is rarely used for home light circuits because when one light bulb fails, all the lights go out on the circuit. A string of old-style Christmas tree lights is an example of series wiring.

CODES AND PERMITS

The *National Electrical Code* (referred to as "*NEC*" or simply "the Code") is a set of rules spelling out wiring methods and materials to be used in electrical work. With safety as its purpose, the *NEC* forms the basis for all regulations and standards applied to electrical installations. Some cities, counties, and states amend the *NEC*; if you move to a new location, check with your municipal building department before beginning any electrical work. This book gives you the practical information you need to work within the framework of the *NEC*.

Local utility company: Your wiring plans may involve a change in electrical service—for example, you may need 240-volt, three-wire service for a new clothes dryer. If so, you must contact your local utility company to obtain the additional service. You should also contact your utility company whenever your building or remodeling plans call for changing the location of your meter and service panel, or when your project will increase your

electrical load. You may avoid trouble later by making sure that your utility company cables are heavy enough for your new load.

Amateur vs. professional electrician: Doing your own electrical work may not always be the best idea. A check with the building department may reveal that your jurisdiction has restrictions on how much and what kinds of electrical wiring a homeowner may do. For instance, you may be able to do all wiring up to the point at which the circuits are connected to the service panel, but the final hookup may have to be done by a licensed electrician.

If things crop up that you don't understand, or if there's some doubt remaining in your mind about your electrical system or any repairs you have done, it's best to call on a professional electrician.

In Canada, wiring requirements may differ from those listed in this book; before beginning any work, check the Canadian Electrical Code.

WORKING SAFELY WITH ELECTRICITY

Electricity is something we all use freely with just a flick of a switch. Electricity is also something to be treated with caution and respect. While these two statements seem to express conflicting viewpoints, together they give a good foundation for working safely with electricity. Once you understand and respect the potential hazards, electrical wiring is quite safe to do.

You can protect yourself from the risk of electrical shock by following some basic safety instructions. Before beginning to work on your wiring, always unscrew the fuse or trip the circuit breaker to the circuit *(page 21)*; if in doubt about what circuit to turn off, shut off the main power supply *(page 20)*.

You've probably heard stories of fires or injuries from causes related to electricity. Barns burn to the ground because of electrical storms, homes are destroyed because of faulty wiring, people get electric shocks—or in extreme cases, are killed—in household electrical accidents. You have no control over electrical storms, but you can and must be careful with electricity in your home.

Several faulty wiring situations can cause fires. For example, restriction of the flow of current through a wire or cord, as when a cord is poorly connected to its plug, may lead to overheating and eventually to a fire. Replace any cord or plug that shows signs of wear and tear. Teach children not to play with cords and plugs, or to stick any object into the slots of receptacles; cap unused receptacles with safety covers that children cannot remove.

Another fire hazard frequently found in homes is the "extension cord octopus," where too many appliances are plugged into an extension cord that isn't hefty enough to carry the electricity these appliances demand. Excessive heat builds up in the cord as it tries to carry the load for all the appliances; the cord's insulation becomes brittle or melts from the heat; wires are exposed as the insulation deteriorates; and eventually a short circuit develops, sending sparks flying when the bare wires touch each other. Too much demand on receptacles and/or extension cords creates a fire hazard.

If you notice a need for more receptacles in your house, you have a couple of options. You can extend an existing circuit, if the circuit is not already overloaded or dedicated to a major appliance, such as a clothes dryer, or you can add a new circuit *(page 54)*.

WHAT CAUSES SHOCKS?

The discussion of circuits on page 17 describes how current flows in a continuous, closed path from the source, through a device that uses the power, and then back to the source. If you accidentally become a link in an electrically live circuit, you'll get a shock. The key word here is "link." To get an electric shock, you must be touching a live wire or device. And, at the same time, you also must be touching a grounded object or another live wire.

It is important to realize that electricity need not flow in wires to make the return trip to the source. It can return to the source through any conducting body—including a person—that contacts the earth directly or touches a conductor that in turn enters the earth.

This may sound like a rather unlikely situation. But consider that whenever you're partially immersed in water, touching any metal plumbing fixture, or standing on the ground or on a damp concrete basement, garage, or patio floor, you're in contact with a grounded object. In other words, you're satisfying one of the two requirements for getting a shock.

There may be two requirements for getting a shock, but there's only one requirement for not getting one: Always make sure that the circuit you intend to work on is dead. Remember—current will pass through, and shock, anyone who becomes a link in an electrically live circuit, as shown below.

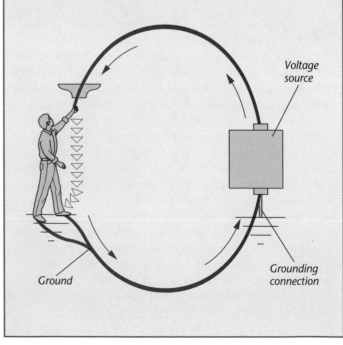

Voltage source

Ground

Grounding connection

SAFEGUARDS IN THE ELECTRICAL SYSTEM

Fuses and circuit breakers, collectively referred to as "overcurrent protection devices," guard electrical systems from damage by too much current.

Whenever wiring is forced to carry more current than it can safely handle—whether it's because of a sudden surge from the utility company, use of too many appliances on one circuit, or a problem within your system —fuses will blow or circuit breakers will trip. Any one of these actions open the circuits, disconnecting the supply of electricity.

A circuit breaker or fuse is inserted into each circuit at the service entrance panel (or in some cases at a subpanel). For adequate protection, the amperage rating of a breaker or fuse must be the same as that of the circuit conductor it protects. For example, a circuit using #12 copper conductor has an ampacity of 20 amperes *(see Table II, page 7)*; the fuse or circuit breaker, therefore, must also be rated for 20 amperes. Never replace any fuse or circuit breaker with one of higher amperage.

A fuse contains a short strip of an alloy with a low melting point. When installed in a socket or fuseholder, the metal strip becomes a link in the circuit. If the amperage flowing in the circuit becomes greater than the rating of the fuse, the metal strip will melt, opening the circuit; the fuse is blown and must be replaced, as shown in the illustration at right.

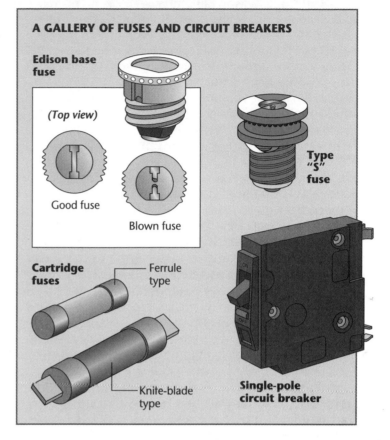

A GALLERY OF FUSES AND CIRCUIT BREAKERS

Edison base fuse

(Top view)

Good fuse

Blown fuse

Type "S" fuse

Cartridge fuses

Ferrule type

Knife-blade type

Single-pole circuit breaker

MORE SAFETY PRECAUTIONS

With the electricity turned off, electrical work can be performed safely. Still, it's a good idea to keep a few additional precautions in mind.

• Remember that water and electricity don't mix. Never work on wiring, fixtures, switches, or appliances in damp or wet conditions. Lay down dry boards to stand on if the floor or ground is wet, and wear rubber boots *(right)*.

• Leave a note on the service panel to alert others that you are working on circuit wiring. Better still—lock it.

• Study how your particular home is wired before you modify or work on the electrical system. The procedures described in this book are based on the assumption that the existing wiring was done correctly.

• Circuits are dead only past the points where they have been opened or disconnected. The lines from the utility company in the service panel are still hot, even after the fuses are removed or the circuit breakers turned off.

• Make sure any circuit you intend to work on is dead; test to confirm the power is off before making any repairs or wire connections.

Edison base fuses: Equipped with screw-in bases like those of ordinary light bulbs, Edison base fuses come in ratings up to 30 amps. According to the National Electrical Code, Edison base fuses are now permitted only as replacements in 120-volt circuits. (This Code restriction is meant to encourage everyone to use the safer Type "S" fuse.) Always match fuse size to circuit rating. For instance, if the circuit is rated for 15 amps, use a 15-amp fuse, not a 20-amp one.

Type "S" fuses: You must install the adapter with the correct rating in the fuse socket before using a Type "S" fuse. Each adapter is constructed so that it is impossible to install a fuse with a higher rating. Fuses can be replaced as needed, but once an adapter is installed, it can't be removed. Type "S" fuses are required in all new installations that use fuses to protect 120-volt circuits.

Cartridge fuses: There are two basic styles of cartridge fuses: ferrule and knife-blade. Ferrule type fuses, which come in ratings of 10 to 60 amps, are usually used to protect the circuit of an individual 120/240-volt appliance, such as a range. Available in ratings of 70 amps or more and suitable for 240 volts, knife-blade fuses are generally used as the main overcurrent protection in fused service entrance panels. A fuse pulling tool *(page 5)* is best for removing cartridge fuses from their fuseholders.

Circuit breakers: Resembling a light switch, a circuit breaker serves both as a switch and as a fuse. As a switch, a circuit breaker lets you open a circuit (turn switch to OFF) whenever you want to work on the wiring. As a fuse, it provides automatic overcurrent protection.

When a breaker is installed in a circuit breaker panel, a bimetallic strip becomes a link in the circuit. Heat from excessive current will bend the metal strip, causing a release to trip and break the circuit. (The toggle goes to OFF or to an intermediate position when this happens.)

Unlike fuses that work on the self-destruct principle, circuit breakers can be reset (turned back on) once they've tripped. All circuit breakers are rated for a specific amperage. As with fuses, the amp rating of a breaker must match the ampacity of the circuit it protects.

THE SERVICE PANEL

Though the ultimate capabilities are usually the same, the exact location and type of service equipment vary from home to home. The service panel might be on the outside of your home, below the meter, or on an inside wall, often directly behind the meter. It might have a single main disconnect, or it could have as many as six switches controlling disconnection. Also, the service entrance panel may or may not contain branch circuit overcurrent protection devices. Variations also occur in the type of overcurrent protection devices. Some systems use circuit breakers; others use fuses.

Because of this variation, don't be concerned if the drawings at right do not match your service panel. The principles of safety and protection are the same regardless of the location and type of service equipment.

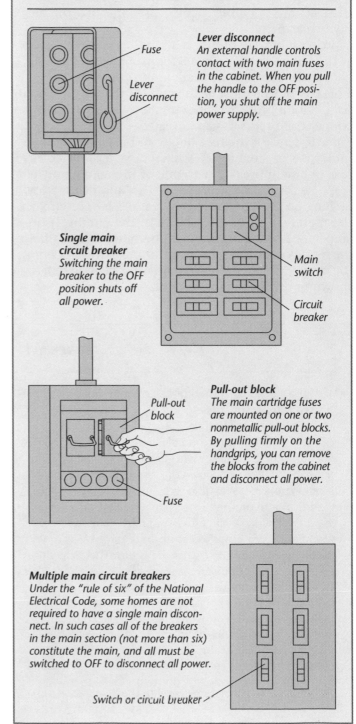

SHUTTING OFF THE MAIN POWER SUPPLY

Most service panels have a switch that can disconnect the entire electrical supply instantly. This shut-off mechanism, also called the "main disconnect," is a vital safety feature whenever you work on existing wiring or make major repairs—or in case of an emergency, such as a fire. The illustrations below show the main types of main disconnects, usually identified as "Main" on the service panel.

Fuse

Lever disconnect

Lever disconnect
An external handle controls contact with two main fuses in the cabinet. When you pull the handle to the OFF position, you shut off the main power supply.

Single main circuit breaker
Switching the main breaker to the OFF position shuts off all power.

Main switch

Circuit breaker

Pull-out block

Fuse

Pull-out block
The main cartridge fuses are mounted on one or two nonmetallic pull-out blocks. By pulling firmly on the handgrips, you can remove the blocks from the cabinet and disconnect all power.

Multiple main circuit breakers
Under the "rule of six" of the National Electrical Code, some homes are not required to have a single main disconnect. In such cases all of the breakers in the main section (not more than six) constitute the main, and all must be switched to OFF to disconnect all power.

Switch or circuit breaker

SHUTTING OFF A CIRCUIT

The most important rule for all do-it-yourself electricians is to never work on any electrically "live" circuit, fixture, or appliance.

Before starting any work, disconnect (or "kill") the circuit at its source in the service panel. If the circuits are protected by fuses, removing the appropriate fuse disconnects the circuit from incoming service. If the circuits are protected by circuit breakers, disconnect a circuit by switching its breaker to the OFF position.

To make sure you disconnect the correct circuit, turn on a light that's connected to the circuit before you remove the fuse or turn off the circuit breaker. The light will go out when you've removed the correct fuse or turned off the correct breaker. If you have any doubt about which fuse or breaker protects which circuit, shut off all current coming into your home at the main disconnect, as shown on the previous page.

When you're shutting off power to a circuit at the service panel, spend another moment to prevent a possible disaster. As a safety measure, tape a note on the panel explaining what you're doing so no one will come along and replace the fuse or reset the circuit breaker while you're working on the wiring. Then, either carry the fuse with you in your pocket, tape the circuit breaker in the OFF position, or lock the service panel.

One final step before starting to work is to check that the circuit is actually dead. Plug a lamp or insert a neon tester into the slots of a receptacle on the circuit. If the light or neon tester doesn't glow, the circuit is dead. But if there is light, return to the service panel, and locate the correct fuse or circuit breaker.

When working on a portable electric appliance, such as a lamp, always unplug it first. Just turning off the switch is not enough.

Killing power to a circuit

Removing a plug fuse
In the service panel, locate the plug fuse controlling the circuit you wish to work on. Grasp the fuse by its insulated rim and unscrew it *(right)*. Next, check that electrical devices on the circuit are dead. If they are not, return to the service panel and repeat the procedure until you locate the correct fuse.

Plug fuse

Tripping a circuit breaker
Locate the circuit breaker protecting the circuit you wish to shut off, then push the toggle to the OFF position *(left)*. To reset a tripped circuit breaker, flip the toggle to the ON position. The procedure for resetting a circuit breaker varies. Directions are often embossed on the breaker. Many modern circuit breakers go to an intermediate position between ON and OFF when they trip. To reset, push the toggle firmly to OFF before returning to ON. (Note: switching a circuit breaker may require more force than an ordinary household switch.)

Circuit breaker

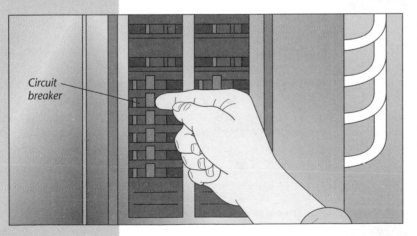

Removing a cartridge fuse
Locate the fuse block protecting the circuit you wish to shut off. Grasp the handle firmly and pull out the fuse block *(right)*. Use a fuse puller or your hand to release the cartridge fuse from the spring clips.

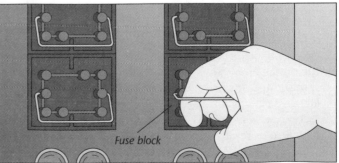

Fuse block

WHAT IF THE LIGHTS GO OUT ?

Problem	It may be . . .	Try this:
Light doesn't go on when you flip the switch	Burned out light bulb (check that another light on the same circuit works)	Replace the bulb with a new one.
Second lamp doesn't light	Dead circuit	Check your service panel for a blown fuse or tripped circuit breaker, indicating a short circuit or an overloaded circuit.
Entire home is without electricity and there are no blown fuses or tripped circuit breakers	If neighboring houses seem to be in the dark too, your area probably has a local power failure	Telephone your utility company.
Your home is the only one in your area without electricity	Main fuse has blown or main circuit breaker has tripped	Check your service panel for a blown fuse or tripped circuit breaker. If the main is intact, call your utility company. You may have a downed line.
House is in partial darkness	Too many lights and appliances on a circuit, causing a fuse to blow or a circuit breaker to trip	Unplug some appliances, then replace the fuse or reset the circuit breaker.

FINDING THE SOURCE OF A SHORT CIRCUIT

When an accidental path is created between a hot wire and any ground, current automatically will flow. This situation is called a "short circuit." The name comes from the fact that the accidental path provides a shorter path to ground than the intended circuit.

An exposed wire spells trouble, whether it's exposed because of worn insulation or a faulty connection. All that has to happen is for the exposed area to touch any grounded object (such as the neutral wire, a grounding wire, a grounded metal box, or grounded metal conduit) and you'll have a short circuit. This is a frequent problem with two-wire cord such as lamp cord. A short circuit will occur whenever the two wires touch each other, since one wire is hot and the other is grounded (neutral).

Most short circuits occur in cords, plugs, and appliances. Look for black smudge marks on faceplates of receptacles and switches, and frayed or charred cords. Replace the damaged cord or plug (page 31) before installing a new fuse or resetting a breaker.

If you find no visible signs of trouble, you'll have to trace your way through the circuit. To do this, turn off all switches and unplug appliances on the dead circuit. Then install a new fuse, or reset the breaker. The following are situations that may occur with instructions of what to do:

If the fuse blows right away, pull it out or make sure the circuit breaker is OFF. Remove each faceplate and inspect the device and wiring. Look for charred wire insulation, a wire shorted against the back of the metal box, or a device literally falling apart. Replace the defective switch or receptacle (page 41) or faulty wiring (page 54). Then install a new fuse or reset the breaker.

If the new fuse doesn't blow or the breaker doesn't trip right away, turn on each wall switch, one by one, until the fuse blows or circuit breaker trips.

If turning on a wall switch causes the fuse to blow or the breaker to trip, the short circuit is in the fixture outlet controlled by the switch, or in the ON position of the switch. With power to the circuit turned off, carefully inspect the outlet and switch for charred wire insulation and faulty connections. Replace the faulty fixture or switch (see page 41). Then install a new fuse or reset the breaker.

If turning on wall switches doesn't blow the fuse or trip the breaker, the trouble is in an appliance. Plug in and turn on the appliances one by one. When the fuse blows or the breaker trips again, you'll know you've found the offending appliance. Then install a new fuse or reset the breaker.

If the circuit went dead as soon as you turned the appliance on, either the appliance or its switch is probably defective and should be repaired or replaced.

If the circuit went dead as soon as you plugged the appliance in, the plug or cord is probably at fault and should be replaced (page 31).

Note: If none of the above solves the problem and your fuse or circuit breaker still blows or trips, your wiring is at fault. At this point, you should call an electrician to have your home's electrical system inspected.

GROUNDING THE ELECTRICAL SYSTEM

Up to this point the discussion of circuits has disregarded grounding. Instead it has worked with just two wires—a hot and a neutral. Electrical codes now require that every 120-volt circuit have a system of grounding.

This is a preventive measure. Grounding assures that all metal parts of a circuit that you might come in contact with are maintained at zero voltage because they are connected directly to the earth. During normal operation the grounding system does nothing; in the event of a malfunction, however, the grounding is there for your protection.

In a typical house circuit, the wiring method dictates how grounding is done. When a home is wired with armored cable, metal conduit, or flexible metal conduit (in which both conduit and fittings are approved for the purpose by the local electrical code), the conductive metal enclosures can themselves form the grounding system. When metal enclosures are not used, a separate grounding wire must be run with the circuit wires. Running a separate grounding wire isn't as complicated as it may sound because nonmetallic sheathed cable contains a bare grounding wire *(page 6)*.

Safeguarding against electrical shock

Circuit breaker

Neutral wire

Hot wire

Ground

Hot bus bars

Metal fixture and pull chain electrically charged

Hot wire accidentally slipped off terminal

Creating a short circuit

If, for instance, a hot wire accidentally became dislodged from a fixture terminal and came into contact with the metal canopy of the light fixture, the fixture and pull chain would become electrically charged, or "hot." If you were to touch the chain or fixture under these conditions, a short circuit could occur in which you would provide the path to ground for the electric current. In other words, you would get a shock *(left)*. This same situation could occur in any number of places where electricity and conductive materials are together—in power tools and appliances with metal housings; in metal switch, junction, and outlet boxes; and in metal faceplates.

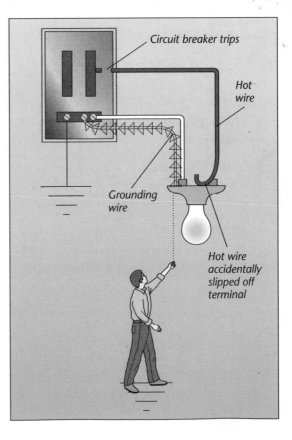

Circuit breaker trips

Hot wire

Grounding wire

Hot wire accidentally slipped off terminal

Preventing electrical shocks
The shock in the example shown above could have been prevented if the circuit had had a grounding system as shown at right. A grounding wire connecting the neutral bus bar to the metal housing of the light fixture would provide an auxiliary electrical path to ground in the event of a short circuit. This grounding wire would carry the fault current back to the distribution center and assure that the fuse or circuit breaker protecting the circuit would trip, or open, shutting off all current flow.

AN INTRODUCTION TO THE BASICS 23

Grounding in metal boxes

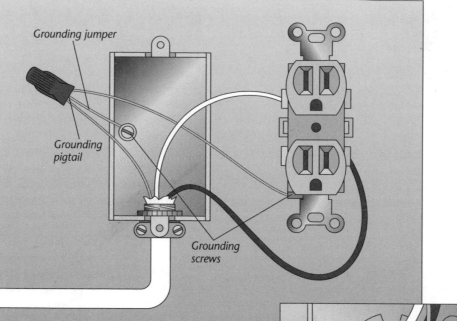

Grounding jumper

Grounding pigtail

Grounding screws

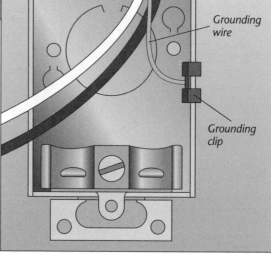

Grounding wire

Grounding clip

Maintaining the grounding pathway

Metal boxes must be grounded; a separate grounding wire in nonmetallic cable provides the path for ground. When installing a switch, self-grounding receptacle, or light fixture in the last box of a circuit run, attach the grounding wire directly to the grounding screw in the back of the box or use a grounding clip to bond the grounding wire to the box *(right)*. If the box is not at the end of a circuit or the receptacle has a grounding terminal, make a grounding jumper using a short piece of wire. Twist together the grounding wires and the jumper wire and secure them with a wire nut *(above)* or a compression sleeve.

Grounding in non-metallic boxes

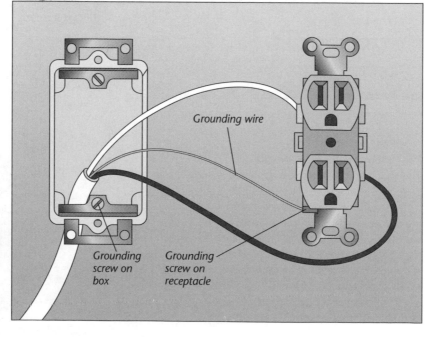

Grounding wire

Grounding screw on box

Grounding screw on receptacle

Dealing with non-metallic boxes

Since nonmetallic boxes don't conduct electricity, they need not be grounded. However, the receptacle must be grounded. If the box is at the end of the circuit, attach the grounding wire of the nonmetallic cable directly to the grounding screw on the receptacle *(left).* Other possible situations are shown opposite.

Grounding a receptacle in the middle of a circuit (grounding terminal)

If the box is in the middle of a circuit run, two (or more) cables enter the box. To ground the device, make a grounding jumper using a short piece of wire the same size as the circuit grounding wires. Attach the grounding jumper to the grounding screw on the device, then twist together the grounding wires and the jumper wire and secure them with a wire nut, as shown at right.

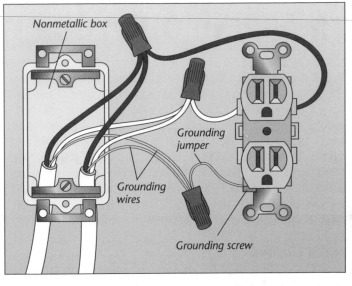

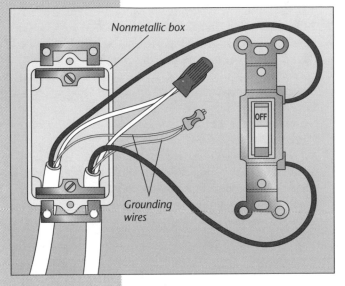

Grounding a switch in the middle of a circuit

Many switches have grounding terminals, which are grounded in the same way as receptacles with grounding terminals. If the switch does not have a grounding terminal, twist together the grounding wires from the two cables entering the box and secure them with a wire nut or a compression sleeve (above).

Grounding fixture boxes

If a fixture box is at the end of the circuit, attach the cable grounding wire to the bar (right). If the fixture is in the middle of a circuit, make up a grounding jumper to join the grounding bar to the cable grounding wires. The light fixture will automatically be grounded when attached to the grounded box. (Some chain-hung fixtures have a separate grounding wire. Join it to the circuit grounding wire and a jumper.)

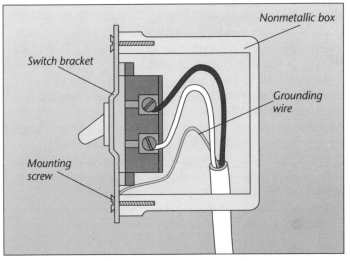

Grounding a switch at the end of a circuit

If your switch is at the end of the circuit and the switch does not have a grounding terminal, secure the grounding wire from the cable entering the box with the mounting screw, placing the wire between the switch bracket and the box (above).

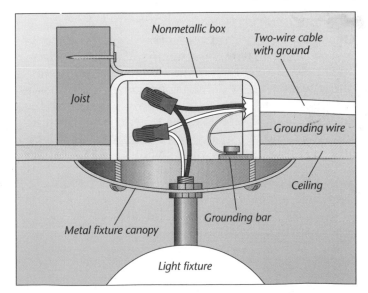

What do I have to work with? This is the first question you should ask yourself when you consider any repairs, alterations, or additions to your present electrical system. The first step in evaluating your electrical system is to determine what type of electrical service you have. Looking through the glass window of your electricity meter, you'll see several numbers printed on the faceplate. The designation "120V" indicates two-wire service; "240V" indicates three-wire service with both 120-volt and 240-volt capabilities.

SERVICE RATINGS

Any electrical system is rated for the maximum amount of current (measured in amperes) it can carry. This rating, determined by the size of the service entrance equipment, is called the "service rating." Keeping you within the bounds of your service rating is the job of the main fuses or circuit breaker.

Service ratings have increased through the years to accommodate greater electrical demands and higher safety standards. Today, the minimum service rating of most new homes is 100 amps. Depending to a large extent on the age of your home, your service rating could be as low as 30 amps or as high as 400 amps. In between the two extremes are the following common service ratings: 60, 100, 125, 150, and 200 amps.

The best way to find out your service rating is to look at the main disconnect, if you have one. Whether it is a breaker or fuses (page 20), the service rating will usually be stamped on the main fuses or circuit breaker.

If your system doesn't have a main disconnect, call the utility company or your local building inspection department rather than trying to figure out the service rating. Someone from either of those two offices will be able to advise you about the rating of your service.

INDIVIDUAL CIRCUITS

Once you've established your service rating, you should make a list of all lamps and lighting fixtures, switches, and appliances on each of the circuits. The illustration opposite shows how to map your home's wiring. If the circuits are not identified on the service panel or if the labeling is out of date, take the time to enter them so that when you're working on your wiring, you will be able to kill power to the right circuit.

POINTS TO REMEMBER WHEN TESTING 120-VOLT CIRCUITS:

• *Make sure the lamp you use for testing works and is turned on.*

• *Make sure to test both ends of a duplex receptacle.*

• *Don't forget to test the switches on any garbage disposal units or dishwashers.*

• *Once the 120-volt circuits are charted, go on to the 240-volt circuits. These circuits—identified in your service panel by a double circuit breaker or a pull-out fuse block with cartridge fuses—go to individual high-wattage appliances such as an electric range, clothes dryer, water heater, heating system, or central air conditioner. Trace the 240-volt circuits by disengaging one overcurrent protection device at a time and finding out which appliance doesn't work.*

• *If the label on your service panel has not been filled in, or if you suspect it may be incorrect or out-of-date, map each circuit in your house following the procedure outlined on the opposite page, then record the information at the service panel.*

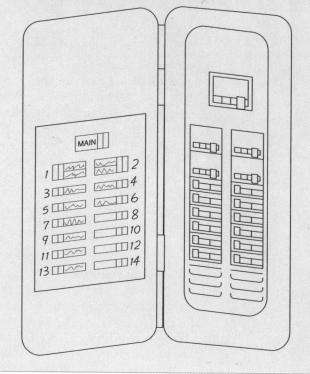

Using numbers and electrical symbols, you can make up a good working drawing of your electrical system. Such a drawing or map can save you much time, whether you plan to wire a new home, alter existing wiring, or trou-bleshoot a problem. The following is a circuit map of a typical two-bedroom house. Note that the dashed lines indicate which switch controls which fixture; they do not show wire routes.

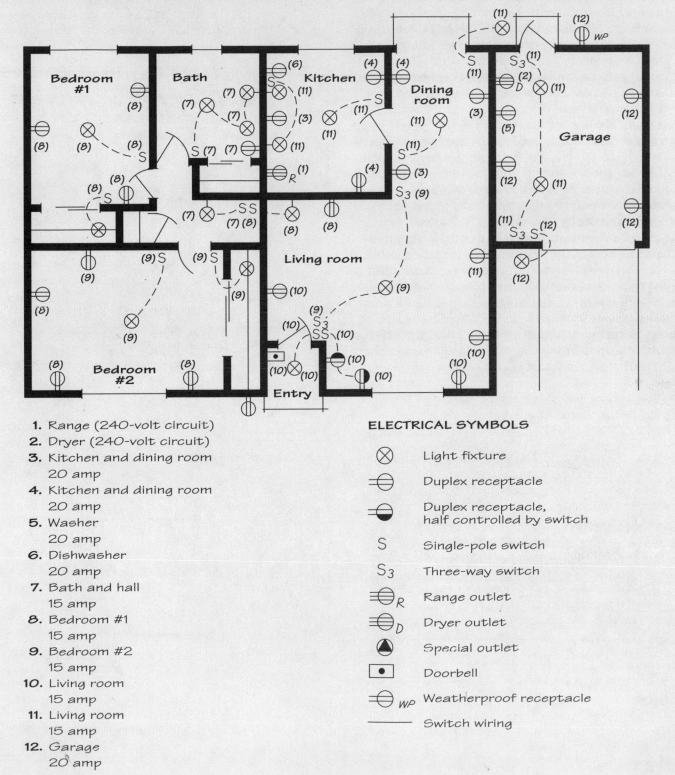

1. Range (240-volt circuit)
2. Dryer (240-volt circuit)
3. Kitchen and dining room
   20 amp
4. Kitchen and dining room
   20 amp
5. Washer
   20 amp
6. Dishwasher
   20 amp
7. Bath and hall
   15 amp
8. Bedroom #1
   15 amp
9. Bedroom #2
   15 amp
10. Living room
   15 amp
11. Living room
   15 amp
12. Garage
   20 amp

ELECTRICAL SYMBOLS

⊗	Light fixture
⊖	Duplex receptacle
⊖	Duplex receptacle, half controlled by switch
S	Single-pole switch
S₃	Three-way switch
⊖ R	Range outlet
⊖ D	Dryer outlet
▲	Special outlet
⊡	Doorbell
⊖ WP	Weatherproof receptacle
—	Switch wiring

CALCULATING ELECTRICAL USAGE

After mapping out your home's wiring circuits, the next step is to determine your present usage, or electrical load. This would be a time-consuming task if you had to go around the house and add up all the wattages of the lights and appliances. However, after considerable research the *National Electrical Code* has established certain values that represent typical electrical usage.

Three watts per square foot (using outside dimensions) of living space and space for future use is the figure used for general purpose circuits (general lighting and receptacles). A nominal value of 1,500 watts is used for each 20-amp small appliance circuit (circuits that power receptacles in the kitchen, dining room, family room, breakfast room, and pantry) and for a laundry circuit at right.

Applying these values to your own home, and using the actual nameplate values of major appliances, you can use one of several formulas to calculate your electrical load. One formula for homes with 120/240-volt service of 100 amps or more is presented as a worksheet at right.

To show how to use the formula, let's take the example of a house with 1,800 square feet (outside dimensions) of finished living space and space adaptable for future use. The house has the usual two small appliance circuits, a laundry circuit, a hot water heater (5,500 watts), a dryer (5,600 watts), a dishwasher (1,500 watts), a garbage disposal (600 watts), a range (15,000 watts), and a central air conditioner (5,000 watts).

The first step is to multiply 1,800 square feet by 3 watts per square foot. The total is 5,400 watts for lighting and general purpose circuits. Add 3,000 watts for the small appliance circuits plus 1,500 watts for the laundry circuit for a total of 9,900 watts. Next, add in the nameplate values of all the major appliances, except the air condition-

---

ASK A PRO

WHAT IF I HAVE LESS THAN 100-AMP SERVICE?

If your service rating is less than 100 amps, you can't use the formula given in the table (right) to calculate your load. You can, however, use a different formula that incorporates the same NEC values for typical usage. Therefore, the general purpose circuits, small appliance circuits, and laundry circuits are computed exacly as they are in the first three entries of the table.

Once you have figured the general purpose circuit load (3 watts x number of square feet of living area), add 1,500 watts for each 20-amp small appliance circuit and laundry circuit. Using this total, take the first 3,000 watts at 100 percent and the balance over 3,000 watts at 35 percent: [3,000 + 0.35 (total — 3,000)].

Add to this value the nameplate rating of all major appliances (space heater, garbage disposal, dishwasher, etc.). This gives you your estimated load in watts. You can find the current by dividing the total wattage by your voltage—120 volts for two-wire service or 240 volts for three-wire service.

HOW TO DETERMINE YOUR ELECTRICAL LOAD

A quick way to estimate your load:

(120/240-volt service of 100 amps or more)

_____ sq. ft. of living area (outside dimensions)
× 3 watts per sq. ft. =   _____ watts

_____ 20-amp small appliance circuits
× 1,500 watts =   _____ watts

Laundry circuit (1,500 watts)   _____ watts

Appliance nameplate values (if values are given in amps, multiply by volts to get watts)
  water heater   _____ watts
  dryer   _____ watts
  dishwasher   _____ watts
  garbage disposal   _____ watts
  range   _____ watts
  other   _____ watts
Add all entries. Total =   _____ watts

Take 40% of the amount over 10,000 watts.
  Subtract 10,000 watts.   −10,000 watts
  difference =   _____ watts
  0.40 × difference =   _____ watts

Find subtotal by adding 10,000 to amount
computed above.   +10,000 watts
  subtotal =   _____ watts

Air conditioner or heater(s) (whichever has the largest value)   _____ watts

Add the last two lines.
  YOUR ESTIMATED LOAD =   _____ watts

Convert load to current by dividing by 240 volts.
  estimated load in
  watts ÷ 240 volts =   _____ amps

er, for a total of 38,100 watts. The next step is to multiply 40 percent by the amount over 10,000 watts (0.40 x 28,100 = 11,240 watts). Adding the 10,000 watts to the 11,240 watts gives a subtotal of 21,240 watts.

The final step is to add the 5,000 watts of the air conditioner. This gives a grand total of 26,240 watts.

In terms of current, dividing the grand total of 26,240 watts by 240 volts comes to 109.33 amps. The service rating for the sample house, therefore, should be 125 amps or higher.

To calculate your electrical load, enter the values appropriate to your home in the worksheet provided on the facing page, then compare the total load with your present service rating. If the two values are close together, your present service cannot accommodate the addition of many new loads; turn to page 54.

TYPICAL WATTAGES AT A GLANCE

Appliance	Watts	Appliance	Watts	Appliance	Watts
Air conditioner, central	5,000	Garbage disposal	300-900	Refrigerator, standard	720
Air conditioner, room	800-1,600	Hair dryer,		Roaster	1,425
Blender	350-1,000	hand-held	260-1,500	Sander, portable	540
Broiler	1,000-1,500	Heater, built-in		Saw, circular	1,200
Can opener	100-216	(baseboard)	1,600	Sewing machine	75-150
Coffee grinder	85-132	Heater, portable	1,000-1,500	Shaver	12
Coffee maker	850-1,625	Heating pad	75	Soldering iron	150
Computer	125-200	Heat lamp	250	Steam iron	1,100
Computer, printer	125-200	Lamps, fluorescent		Stereo, hi-fi	
Corn popper	600	(per bulb)	15-75	compact disc player	12-15
Dishwasher	1,080-1,800	Lamps, incandescent		receiver	420
Drill, portable	360	(per bulb)	25-200	turntable	12
Dryer, clothes	5,600-9,000	Lamps, halogen	20-50	turntable-receiver	50-75
Fan, exhaust		Microwave oven	975-1,575	Sunlamp	300
(for range)	176	Mixer, portable	150	Telephone	
Fan, portable	100	Mixer, stand	225	answering machine	10-12
Fan, ceiling	150	Projector,		Television, color	300
Fax machine	125-200	movie or slide	350-500	Toaster	800-1,600
Food processor	200	Radio	100	Trash compactor	1,250
Freezer, frostless	1,056	Range	8,000-15,000	Vacuum cleaner	250-800
Freezer, standard	720	Range, cooktop	4,000-8,000	VCR	17-23
Frying pan	1,250-1,465	Range, oven	4,000-8,000	Washer, clothes	840
Furnace, fuel-fired	800	Refrigerator, frostless	960-1,200	Water heater	4,000-6,000

PLAY IT SAFE

READING A LABEL

Do not overload a circuit by exceeding its amperage rating. To determine its electrical load, list all the fixtures and appliances and add up their wattage ratings. Look for a small plate affixed to back or bottom of the appliances (right); wattage ratings for lighting fixtures are located on a sticker near the socket. To convert watts to calculate the wattage, use the formula volt x amperes = watts. In this example: 120v x 21 amps = 252 watts.

REPAIRING CORDS, PLUGS, LIGHTS, AND DOORBELLS

Although some electrical work, such as making connections at the service entrance, requires the expertise of a qualified electrician, you don't need the know-how of an expert to undertake basic electrical repairs in your home.

Many of these repairs and improvements should be done as preventive maintenance. Don't wait until a defect causes a fire or short circuit before taking remedial action. Periodically, inspect the plugs and cords on your lamps and appliances for signs of wear and tear. Look for cracked or frayed insulation along the length of the cord, especially where the cord attaches to the plug and to the lamp or appliance. Also inspect the plug for damage. A cord with badly frayed or brittle insulation is a hazard. It should be thrown away and replaced, not temporarily repaired. Always replace any plug that has loose or bent prongs.

If a bulb flickers or does not light when you turn on an incandescent lamp or lighting fixture, first check that the bulb is not loose or burned out. Then, check the contact tab in the base of the socket. If the tab is too flat, it will not make contact with the base of the bulb. Use a standard screwdriver to pry it up slightly *(page 35)*. If the contact tab is broken, replace the socket *(page 34)*.

This chapter also provides you with step-by-step instructions for remedying common problems with fluorescent fixtures—how to replace burned out fluorescent tubes, tubeholders, and ballasts. You'll also find out how to diagnose and correct low-voltage doorbell systems.

Electrical work is safe as long as you make sure the current is off before working on any wiring. This means unplugging a lamp, or shutting off the circuit at the service panel *(page 21)*.

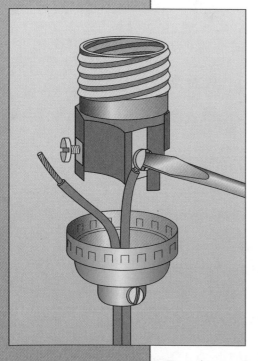

To make sound wire connections at a socket, hook the wire end clockwise around the screw terminal and tighten the screw.

REPLACING CORDS AND PLUGS

Danger signs on cords and plugs include arcing electricity, irregularly transmitted electricity, physical damage, and excessive heat (a cord or plug that's too warm to touch). If the cord shows signs of damage (frayed or cracked insulation), replace the entire length of cord. Detach the cord from the lamp or appliance, and take the old cord with you to an electrical supply store. Buy a length of replacement cord the same wire gauge as the old one. The inventory at right shows typical flexible cord for lamps, appliances, and power tools. Do not use flexible cord as a permanent extension of fixed wiring.

As a rule of thumb, when you are replacing a defective cord, also replace the plug. Always replace a plug that has bent, loose, or missing prongs, or damaged casing. There are two common kinds of plugs: those that are self-connecting and those that have screw terminals. The step-by-step instructions below describe how to attach both kinds of plugs.

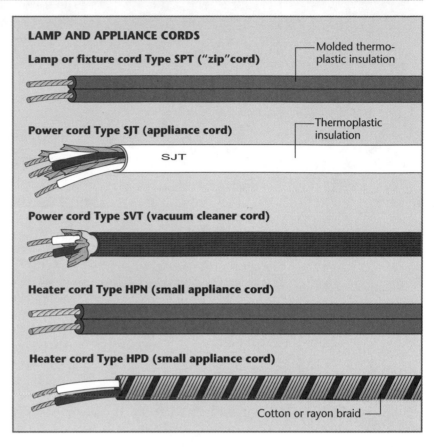

LAMP AND APPLIANCE CORDS

Lamp or fixture cord Type SPT ("zip"cord)

Molded thermo-plastic insulation

Power cord Type SJT (appliance cord)

Thermoplastic insulation

SJT

Power cord Type SVT (vacuum cleaner cord)

Heater cord Type HPN (small appliance cord)

Heater cord Type HPD (small appliance cord)

Cotton or rayon braid

Replacing a self-connecting plug

TOOLKIT
- Diagonal-cutting pliers
- Standard screwdriver (optional)

1 ▶ Inserting the zip cord
Trim the end of the zip cord so that the ends are even; do not separate the wires. Separate the plug cover from the plug core; if necessary, pry a standard screwdriver between the plug cover and the core. Slide the cover onto the cord. Spread apart the prongs, and push the zip cord into the plug core as far as the cord will go *(right)*.

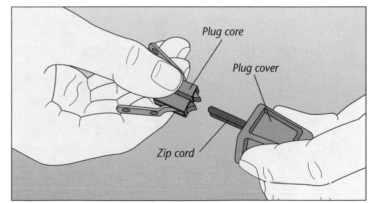

Plug core

Plug cover

Zip cord

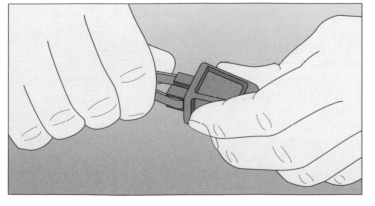

◀ 2 Attaching the plug
Squeeze the prongs together, piercing the cord and securing it to the plug core. Next, slide the plug cover over the plug core *(left)*. Note: Some self-connecting plug covers do not slide off the plug core. Lift the lever on the top of the plug, insert the zip cord, and press down on the lever to secure the cord.

Wiring a screw terminal plug

TOOLKIT
- Diagonal-cutting pliers (optional)
- Utility knife
- Wire strippers
- Long-nose pliers
- Screwdriver

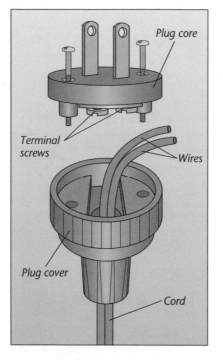

Plug core

Terminal screws

Wires

Plug cover

Cord

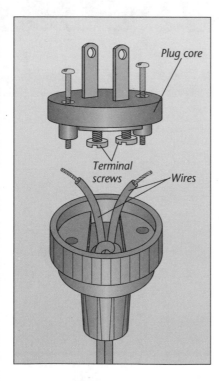

Plug core

Terminal screws

Wires

1 Preparing the new plug
Use diagonal-cutting pliers or a utility knife to cut off the defective plug. (If the cord is frayed or cracked, replace it, too.) Unscrew and remove the new plug's core. With the cord on a flat work surface, use a utility knife to split the end of the cord to separate it into two wires approximately 8" long. Push the cord through the plug cover (left).

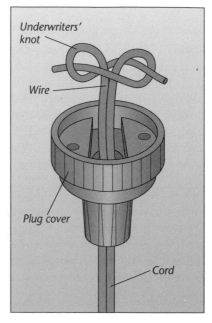

Underwriters' knot

Wire

Plug cover

Cord

2 Making an Underwriters' knot
Make a loop with each of the wires, then pass the end of each wire through the other loop. Pull tightly on the wires to form an Underwriters' knot (right). This prevents strain on the terminal screws when the plug is pulled from a receptacle. (When removing a plug, always grasp the plug, not the cord.)

3 Preparing the wire ends
Using wire strippers, remove $1/2$" to $3/4$" of insulation from the wire ends, being careful not to nick the wires. (If you nick the wires, snip off the damaged wire end, and begin again.) Twist each stranded wire end in a clockwise direction, then unscrew the screw terminals on the plug core to allow space for the wires.

4 Attaching the cord to the plug
Form loops with each wire end; wrap each loop clockwise three-quarters of the way around a screw terminal on the plug core. Use a screwdriver to tighten the terminal screws (right); if necessary, trim excess wire from the wire ends. Fit the plug core onto the plug cover and tighten the screws.

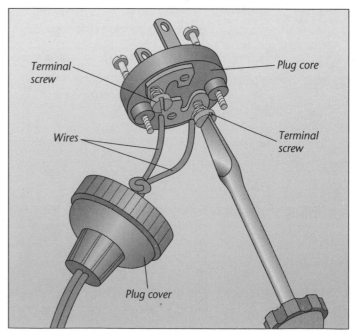

Terminal screw

Plug core

Wires

Terminal screw

Plug cover

When purchasing a replacement plug, take the defective plug with you to the store to ensure that you get the same kind. If your receptacles have one wide slot and one narrow slot, buy a polarized plug—one with a narrow prong and a wide prong. When wiring a polarized plug, connect the marked wire of the cord (indicated by thin band of color, ribbing, or a colored strand visible in the wire ends) to the wide prong and the unmarked wire to the narrow prong. This safety feature ensures that the switch impedes the current-carrying wire, and not the neutral wire, reducing the chances of getting a shock. Electric current will not flow through the lamp when the switch is turned off.

Many plugs now have three prongs—a wide prong, a narrow prong, and a U-shaped prong. When wiring a three-prong plug, follow the procedure for wiring a two-prong plug, attaching the green wire to the green screw terminal on the plug.

Although appliance plugs look slightly different from plugs found on lamps, they are wired in the same way.

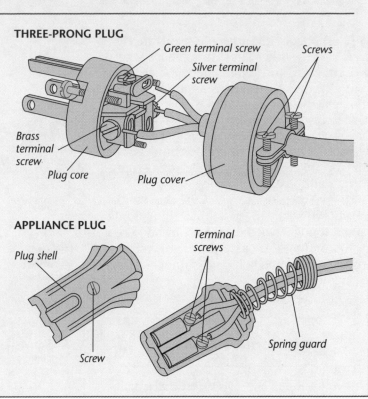

THREE-PRONG PLUG
Green terminal screw
Silver terminal screw
Screws
Brass terminal screw
Plug core
Plug cover

APPLIANCE PLUG
Terminal screws
Plug shell
Spring guard
Screw

REPAIRING LAMPS

Most plug-in incandescent lamps are electrically alike. They all have a socket, switch, cord, and plug. And these are the four elements that may wear out. Replacing the defective part is usually all that is necessary to restore the lamp. Low-voltage lamps have a transformer that also may need to be replaced. On some low-voltage models, you may be able to unscrew the defective transformer and install a new one.

The typical parts of an incandescent lamp are shown in the illustration at right. Some lamps, though, whether they are incandescent or low-voltage, are assembled with rivets instead of nuts and bolts and cannot be taken apart and repaired.

TROUBLESHOOTING A LAMP

If your lamp doesn't work, first check that it is plugged into an active receptacle. Then, diagnose the problem by taking the following steps:

Bulb: Make sure the bulb is a good one and that it is screwed into the socket as far as it will go. Replace the bulb, if necessary.

Cord and plug: Inspect the cord and plug for breaks and frayed areas. If necessary, replace them *(page 31)*.

Socket: Next, clean and adjust the socket tab *(opposite)*. If that doesn't solve the problem, replace the damaged socket.

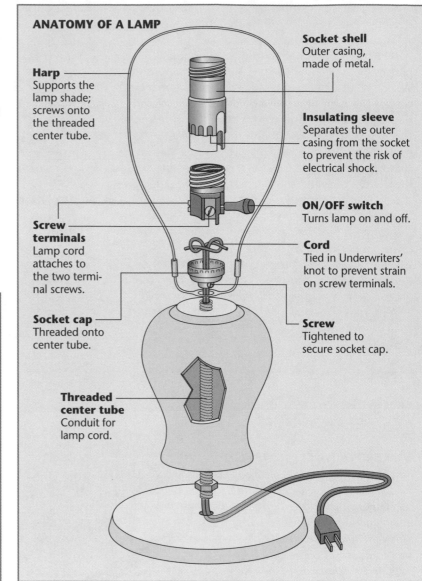

ANATOMY OF A LAMP

Harp
Supports the lamp shade; screws onto the threaded center tube.

Socket shell
Outer casing, made of metal.

Insulating sleeve
Separates the outer casing from the socket to prevent the risk of electrical shock.

ON/OFF switch
Turns lamp on and off.

Screw terminals
Lamp cord attaches to the two terminal screws.

Cord
Tied in Underwriters' knot to prevent strain on screw terminals.

Socket cap
Threaded onto center tube.

Screw
Tightened to secure socket cap.

Threaded center tube
Conduit for lamp cord.

Replacing a lamp socket

TOOLKIT
• Screwdriver

1 ▶ Removing the old socket
Unplug the lamp before doing any work on it. Squeeze the socket shell near the switch, where the word *press* is embossed, and lift it off. Pull off the insulating sleeve, loosen the screw terminals and unhook the wires from the terminals on the socket. Take the old socket along when you buy a new one to assure that you get a proper replacement. The new socket will include a socket cap, but there is often no need to replace the existing one; if so, do not undo the Underwriters' knot. Otherwise, thread the cord through the new socket cap and part the lamp cord 2 1/2" *(right)*.

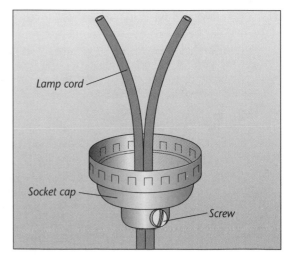

Lamp cord

Socket cap

Screw

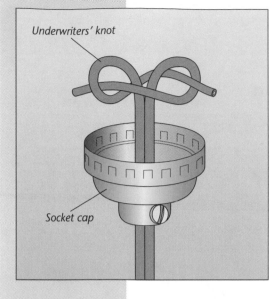

Underwriters' knot

Socket cap

2 ▶ Preparing the wire ends

If you are rewiring a lamp, feed the lamp cord through the socket cap and make an Underwriters' knot by forming a loop with each wire. Pass the end of each wire through the opposite loop *(left)* and pull to tighten the knot. Strip off ¹/₂" to ³/₄" of insulation from the wire ends. Loosen the screw terminals on the socket, but don't force them all the way out.

3 ▶ Making the wire connections

Loop the wires clockwise around the screw terminals of the new socket and tighten the screws *(right)*. Place the insulating sleeve over the socket and then put on the socket shell. Make sure that the corrugated edges of the shell fit inside the rim of the cap, and then push them together until you hear the shell click into place. Squeeze the arms of the harp together and slide them into the retainer.

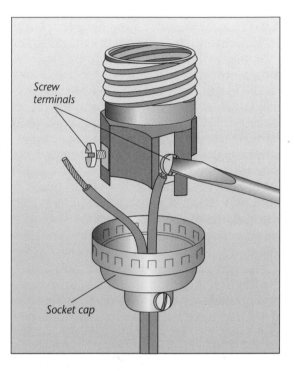

Screw terminals

Socket cap

HOW TO REWIRE A LAMP

Take a close look at your lamp before you remove the old cord completely. If the cord twists or curves inside the lamp, you might want to use the following method of feeding the new cord through:

1. Remove the socket shell, insulating sleeve, and wires from the screw terminals, then untie the Underwriters' knot.

2. Working at the socket end of the lamp, attach the new cord to the old cord by stripping off about ³/₄ inch of insulation from the new cord and twisting the wires of the two cords together. A few turns of tape over the twisted wires will strengthen the joint and make it less likely to catch on its way through the lamp base.

3. Gently pry up any baize covering from the base of the lamp.

4. Pulling carefully on the old cord, thread the new cord through the lamp. When the new cord is in place, remove the tape, and detach the old cord.

5. Connect the new cord to the socket *(above)*, and reassemble the socket.

6. Purchase a replacement plug and connect it to the other end of the new cord, as described on pages 31 to 33. If necessary, use a dab of glue to reattach the baize to the base of the lamp.

QUICK FIX

CLEANING AND ADJUSTING THE SOCKET TAB

If a lamp doesn't work, check that it is plugged in, and that the bulb is not loose or burned out. If you still have not solved the problem, unplug the lamp, unscrew the bulb, and inspect the socket tab. If the tab is too flat, it will not make contact with the base of the bulb. To raise the socket tab, use a standard screwdriver to gently pry it up, as shown. Also use the tip of the screwdriver to scrape dirt from the tab. If the lamp still does not work, replace the socket (facing page).

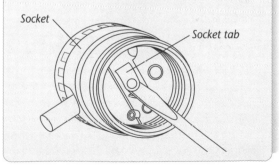

Socket

Socket tab

FIXING FLUORESCENT LIGHTS

Bulb for bulb and watt for watt, a fluorescent light provides more light for your money than an incandescent light does. For example, a 40-watt fluorescent tube produces almost six times as much light as a 40-watt incandescent bulb. And the fluorescent tube will last about five times as long as the incandescent bulb. Fluorescent fixtures are a good lighting option for kitchens and workshops where bright light is required for extended periods of time.

Unlike the simple principle of an incandescent bulb, which glows when current flows through the filament, an intricate electrical process takes place before a fluorescent tube gives off light.

The two most common types of fluorescent light fixtures for homes are rapid-start and preheat. It is easy to distinguish between them because the starter mechanism of the rapid-start type is built right into the ballast; on the preheat type, each tube has a visible starter unit, as shown in the illustration at right. The starters, which look like small aluminum cylinders, tend to burn out as often as the bulbs do.

A third type, less commonly used in the home, is the instant-start. This type has no starter and is distinguished by a tube with a single pin on each end.

Tubes, starters, ballasts, and tubeholders are the components usually involved in fluorescent lamp repair. All components are easy to replace, making most repairs a matter of substitution.

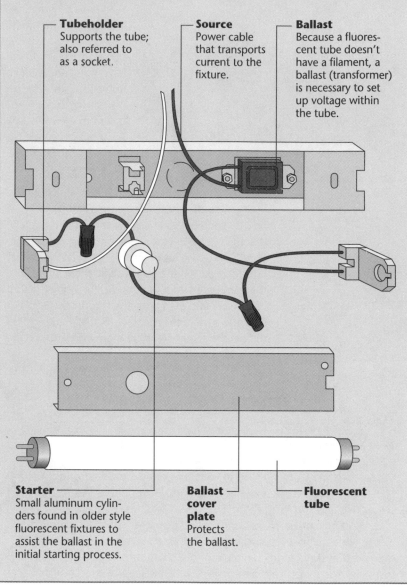

A TYPICAL PREHEAT FIXTURE

Tubeholder
Supports the tube; also referred to as a socket.

Source
Power cable that transports current to the fixture.

Ballast
Because a fluorescent tube doesn't have a filament, a ballast (transformer) is necessary to set up voltage within the tube.

Starter
Small aluminum cylinders found in older style fluorescent fixtures to assist the ballast in the initial starting process.

Ballast cover plate
Protects the ballast.

Fluorescent tube

![tape measure icon] **ASK A PRO**

WHAT SHOULD I KNOW ABOUT BUYING REPLACEMENT PARTS ?

Replacement parts for a fluorescent lamp, available in most home centers, must be carefully matched to the fixture. Tubes and ballasts can't be interchanged between different types of fixtures, and the starter (if there is one) and ballast must match the wattage of the tube. You'll find most of the information you need printed on the parts themselves. When a fluorescent tube burns out, be sure to purchase a new tube
that is compatible with your fixture. Read the information at the end of your old tube, especially noting its wattage and length.

Tubes are available in a range of temperature ratings: the higher the temperature rating, the warmer the light. To boost the life expectancy of a tube, leave the fixture on for several hours rather than switching it on and off for infrequent use.

TROUBLESHOOTING A FLUORESCENT TUBE

Problem	It may be . . .	Try this:
Lamp won't light	Tube burned out (blackened ends)	Replace tube
	Improper installation	Take out and install again
	Fuse blown or circuit breaker tripped	Replace or reset
	Starter burned out	Replace starter
	Dirty tube (rapid-start only)	Remove tube, wash, rinse, dry, and replace
	Tubeholder broken	Replace tubeholder
	Fixture too cold	Raise temperature to at least 50°F
	Oxide film buildup on tube pins	Remove tube; use sandpaper to clean pins
Lamp flickers (Note: New tubes may flicker a short time after installation.)	Poor contact with tubeholders	Realign tubeholders; straighten and sand tubeholders if necessary
	Improper installation	Take out and install again
	Tube nearly worn out (blackened ends)	Replace tube
	Oxide buildup on tube pins	Remove tube; use sandpaper to clean pin
	Fixture too cold	Raise temperature to at least 50°F
Ends of tube are discolored (Note: Darkened bands about 2 inches from ends are normal.)	Tube almost worn out	Replace tube
	Defective starter (preheat type with new tubes)	Replace starter
One end of tube discolored	Temperamental tube	Remove tube; turn end for end
Ends of tube glow, but center doesn't	Defective starter	Replace starter
Lamp fixture hums	Defective ballast	Replace ballast
	Ballast incorrectly installed	Check wiring on ballast diagram and correct
	Wrong type of ballast	Check wattage and type; replace ballast
	Defective ballast	Replace ballast

Replacing a tube

Tube

Installing a tube

Remove the diffuser, if there is one. To remove a double pin type fluorescent tube, twist it a quarter turn in either direction and gently pull out (left). To install a new tube, push it into the tubeholders and give the tube a quarter turn to lock it in place.

A single pin type tube is removed by pushing it against the spring-loaded tubeholder until the other end of the tube can be removed. To install a single pin type tube, put the tube pin in the tubeholder and push until the other end can be inserted.

For either type, now reinstall the diffuser.

Replacing a ballast

TOOLKIT
- Diagonal-cutting pliers
- Screwdriver or nutdriver
- Multipurpose tool

1 ▶ Disconnecting the wiring

Turn off power to the fluorescent fixture at the service panel and at the wall switch. Remove the tubes and the ballast cover plate to expose the ballast. (In table models, the ballast is located in the base of the lamp.) Remove the wiring connected to the old ballast by cutting all the wires coming out from it about 5" from the ballast using diagonal-cutting pliers *(right)*.

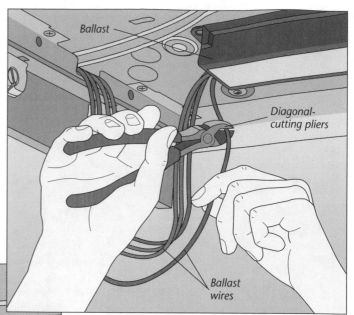

Ballast

Diagonal-cutting pliers

Ballast wires

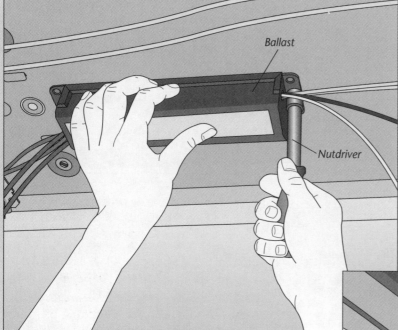

Ballast

Nutdriver

◀ 2 Taking down the ballast

The ballast is secured to the fixture with screws or bolts. To remove the ballast, use one hand to hold it firmly, then undo the mounting screws using a screwdriver or a nutdriver *(left)*. Purchase a replacement socket of the same wattage as the old one; either note the wattage on the ballast or take it with you when you buy the new one.

3 ▶ Installing a new ballast

The new ballast will have about 5" of each wire connected to it. Mount the new ballast before you connect its wires to the wiring in the fixture. To connect the wires, strip about ¹/₂" of insulation from the end of each wire and then use a wire nut for every two wires. Match up the color-coded wires correctly: connect red to red, blue to blue, etc. Check your work against the wiring diagram on the ballast. Reinstall the ballast cover plate, tubes, and diffuser.

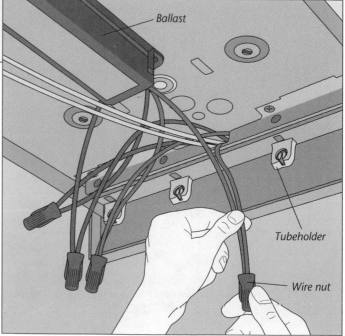

Ballast

Tubeholder

Wire nut

Replacing tube-holders

TOOLKIT
• Screwdriver

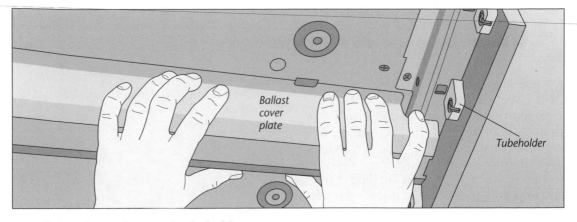

Ballast cover plate

Tubeholder

1 Removing a damaged tubeholder

To gain access to the tubeholders (sometimes called sockets), take off the diffuser, tube, and ballast cover plate (*above*). To remove a tubeholder, disconnect the wires. If the wires are connected by terminal screws, loosen the screws to free the wires. If the tubeholder has push-in wire connectors, release each wire by inserting a small screwdriver or nail into the slot next to the connection. Then remove the tubeholder by taking out the mounting screw on the tubeholder bracket. (On some models you may have to take the end bracket off the fixture to slide off the tubeholder.)

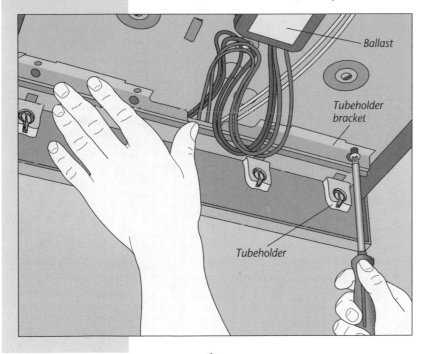

Ballast

Tubeholder bracket

Tubeholder

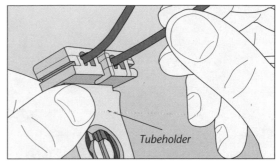

Tubeholder

2 Installing the new tubeholder

Because there is considerable variety in tubeholders, take the one you're replacing with you when buying a new one. First install the tubeholder bracket by setting the mounting screw in place and tightening it (*left*). Next, hook the wires around each terminal screw and tighten them; for push-in type tubeholders, push the wires into the slots (*above*). Reinstall the ballast cover plate, tube, and diffuser, if there is one.

SAFETY TIP

IS THERE ANY DANGER OF GETTING AN ELECTRICAL SHOCK WHEN WORKING ON A FLUORESCENT FIXTURE?

Although fluorescent fixtures have a ballast that initially boosts the incoming voltage, there is no danger of getting a shock if current to the fixture is turned off at the service panel before working on the fixture. With a table-model fluorescent lamp, this means unplugging the lamp. If your fixture is wall or ceiling mounted, you must de-energize the circuit by removing the fuse or tripping the circuit breaker.

Take extra care when disposing of a burned out tube or a broken one; the mercury inside the tube is poisonous. Consult your local environmental protection agency to find out if there are any restrictions concerning the disposal of fluorescent tubes. When disposing of a ballast, make sure it contains no PCBs; this information should be marked on the ballast. If not, also treat the ballast as hazardous waste.

CURING SILENT DOORBELLS

Whether they ring, buzz, or chime, all doorbell systems operate with low voltage—that is, voltage significantly lower than the 120 volts of normal household current. The illustration at right shows how a transformer is wired into a doorbell circuit to step down the 120-volt current to anywhere from 6 to 24 volts, depending on the capacity of the transformer and bell.

For most diagnostic work on your doorbell, you must have the power source connected. However, always de-energize the circuit by pulling the fuse or tripping the breaker if you are going to work on the transformer. (Remember, the input side of the transformer is high voltage—120 volts.)

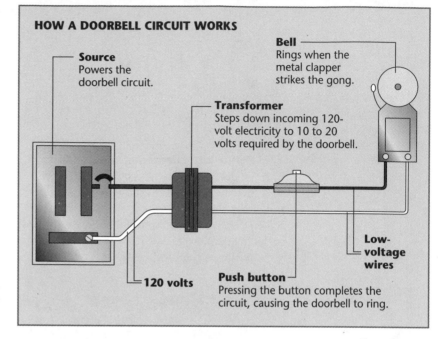

HOW A DOORBELL CIRCUIT WORKS

Source
Powers the doorbell circuit.

Bell
Rings when the metal clapper strikes the gong.

Transformer
Steps down incoming 120-volt electricity to 10 to 20 volts required by the doorbell.

Low-voltage wires

120 volts

Push button
Pressing the button completes the circuit, causing the doorbell to ring.

DIAGNOSING DOORBELL PROBLEMS

When your doorbell doesn't ring or buzz, the first thing to examine is the source of power. Make sure that the fuse or circuit breaker protecting the circuit hasn't blown or tripped. Once you are assured that the 120-volt side of the transformer is getting power, go on to check the low-voltage side.

Transformer: While someone else goes to the door and pushes the button, listen to the transformer. If you hear a humming sound, indicating that the transformer is working, the problem is elsewhere—possibly in the bell mechanism. Follow the advice below to service the bell mechanism. If you don't hear a hum, your transformer could be defective or there could be a break somewhere in the circuit.

Push button: To check that the button is working, disconnect the two wires and touch their bare ends together. If this makes the bell ring, the push button is defective and should be replaced.

Wires: If the push button still does not work, check for a poor or broken wire connection. Because low-voltage wiring uses small wire (usually #18 for doorbells), the wires can break, fray, or lose their insulation. Look for signs of wear; use electrical tape to make any minor repairs to the wires.

Wire connections: Next, carefully check wire connections at the transformer, bell mechanism, and push but-

ton. On some models, you may need to remove the push button cover or unscrew the push button unit from the wall. Using fine sandpaper and a screwdriver, scrape off corrosion from the contacts; clean and tighten any loose terminal connections. If the contacts are flat, use a standard screwdriver to pry them up slightly (below).

Taping wires, cleaning contacts, and tightening connectors are often all that's necessary to fix a silent doorbell.

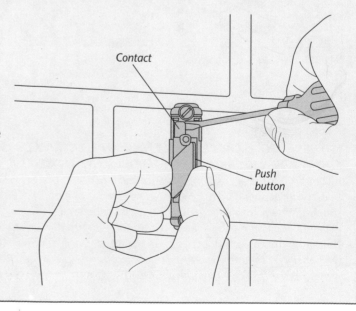

Contact

Push button

SWITCHES AND RECEPTACLES

Switches and receptacles are the electrical workhorses in most homes. Whether they're used to turn on and off lighting fixtures, provide power to a toaster, vacuum cleaner, or home computer, switches and receptacles receive a lot of daily wear and tear. Though they are designed to provide years of reliable service, both of these devices eventually can wear out.

This chapter explains the basic technique of installing switches and receptacles, whether you're replacing a defective one, or upgrading your existing wiring by adding specialized switches and receptacles that better meet your needs. You'll learn about the different switch wiring options and how to install them—from single-pole switches that turn off a light from one location to dimmer switches that allow you to regulate the intensity of the light source. Three-way and four-way switches are useful near stairs and along hallways because they can be turned on and off from two or more locations. When installing a switch, refer to the wiring diagrams on pages 45 and 46 as a guide.

Receptacles range from the standard grounded three-slot type to specialized receptacles that are required for some appliances. You'll learn how to backwire a receptacle *(page 51)*, as well as the advantages of installing a specialized ground fault circuit interrupter that protects you against electrical shocks *(page 49)*.

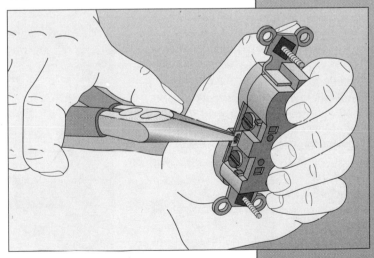

To make the upper and lower outlets of a duplex receptacle operate independently, simply break off the breakoff fin located between the brass screw terminals.

HOW SWITCHES WORK

All switches are rated according to the specific amperage and voltage they are suited for. Switches marked CO-ALR can be used with either copper or aluminum wire. Unmarked switches and those marked CU-AL can be used with copper wire only.

Whether you are replacing an old switch or adding new ones to your home, read the information stamped on your new switch carefully. Make sure the switch you are going to install has the same amperage and voltage ratings as the one you are replacing, or that it is suitable for the circuit.

Most switches in a home are of the single-pole or three-way types. Single-pole switches have two terminals of the same color and a definite right side up. All switches are wired into hot (black) wires only; with a single-pole switch, it makes no difference which hot wire goes to which terminal.

Three-way switches have two terminals of the same color (brass or silver colored) and one of another color (usually black). There is no right side up or upside down with a three-way switch; however, it is important to know which of the three terminals is the odd-colored one. This terminal is often called the common terminal.

PLAY IT SAFE

COLOR CODING—AN EXCEPTION

Up to this point we have assumed that a white wire is always a neutral wire. Wires that are black, red, or any color other than white, green, or gray are always hot. But in some cases, a white wire may substitute as a hot (black) wire. An example of this exception is shown in the switch loop on page 44. In this example, the switch loop is wired with two-wire cable that is purchased with one black wire and one white wire; and the white wire substitutes as the current-carrying wire going from the source to the switch. According to the Code, it is not necessary to reidentify the white wire as a black wire.

CHOOSING A SWITCH

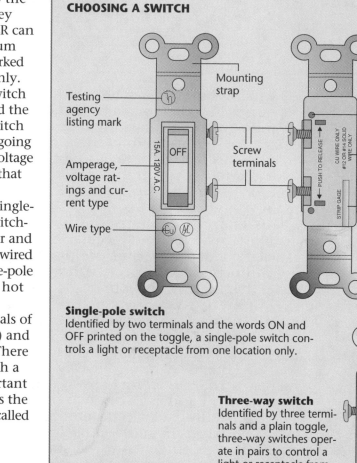

Testing agency listing mark

Mounting strap

Amperage, voltage ratings and current type

Screw terminals

Wire type

Push-in terminals

Wire type

Strip gauge

Single-pole switch
Identified by two terminals and the words ON and OFF printed on the toggle, a single-pole switch controls a light or receptacle from one location only.

Three-way switch
Identified by three terminals and a plain toggle, three-way switches operate in pairs to control a light or receptacle from two locations.

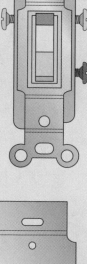

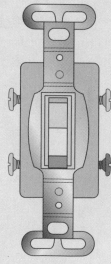

Four-way switch
Identified by four terminals and no ON or OFF indicators on the toggle, a four-way switch is used only in combination with a pair of three-way switches to control a light or receptacle from more than two locations.

Dimmer switch
This switch allows you to get maximum or minimum brightness from a light, or any gradation in between. (Note: Special dimmer switches are required for fluorescent lights.)

Single-pole switch circuits

Circuit complete

Switches turn things on and off by controlling the flow of electric current. The simple knife-blade switch shown below illustrates how a switch closes (completes) a circuit, turning the light on. Though the switches in our homes don't look like the stylized switch in the illustration, they work on the same principle. The important concept to remember is that switches are installed only in hot wires.

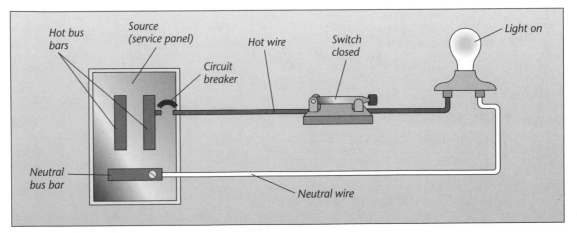

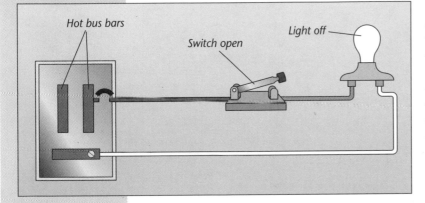

Circuit broken

The switch in a hot wire disconnects the light from the hot bus bar as shown at left. This leaves the light at ground potential (zero volts) and eliminates the possibility of a shock or short circuit at the device when the switch is open. A switch in the neutral wire would also interrupt the flow of current, but it would not disconnect the light from the hot bus bar. As a result, a shock or short circuit at the light would be possible.

Light controlled by a switch

The illustration at right is a more realistic view of the switch circuits discussed above. It shows a light fixture controlled by a single-pole switch. Notice that the black (hot) wires are attached directly to the screw terminals on the switch; the neutral wires bypass the switch and go directly to the light fixture.

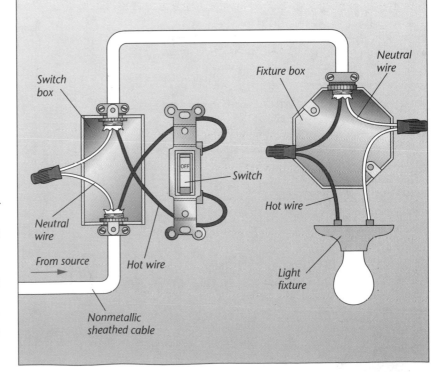

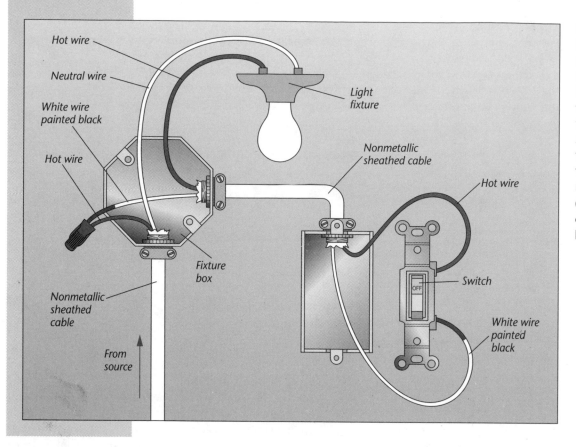

Hot wire

Neutral wire

White wire painted black

Hot wire

Nonmetallic sheathed cable

Fixture box

From source

Light fixture

Nonmetallic sheathed cable

Hot wire

Switch

White wire painted black

Switch loop

Because of code limitations on the number of wires that a given size box may contain, circuit wires sometimes run to the light first, with a switch loop going to the switch. This situation is illustrated at left. Be sure that the black (hot) wire in the cable connects to both the light and the switch.

THREE-WAY SWITCHES

If you want to be able to turn a light on and off at two locations, such as at the top and the bottom of a staircase or at either end of a hallway, consider installing a pair of three-way switches.

Though single-pole and three-way switches look somewhat alike, two features distinguish them. A single-pole switch has two terminals for wire connections and the words "ON" and "OFF" embossed on the toggle. A three-way switch, on the other hand, has three terminals; "ON" and "OFF" are not indicated on the toggle, since the on and off positions may change, depending on the position of the other switch.

In order to clarify the action of three-way switches, the illustrations at right show a pair of them in a simple light circuit. Each switch has three terminals and a movable blade. The light is off when the circuit is open, one switch is up and one down (right, top). Flip either switch so both are up or down (right, bottom), and the circuit is completed; the light is on.

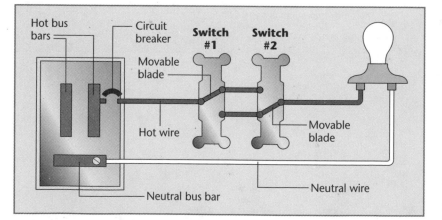

Hot bus bars

Circuit breaker

Switch #1

Switch #2

Movable blade

Hot wire

Movable blade

Neutral wire

Neutral bus bar

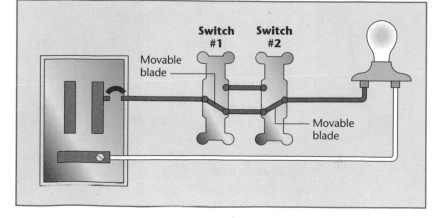

Switch #1

Switch #2

Movable blade

Movable blade

SWITCH WIRING

Wiring single-pole switches

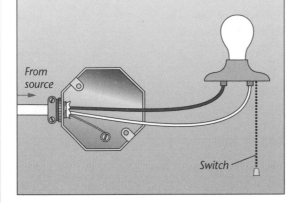

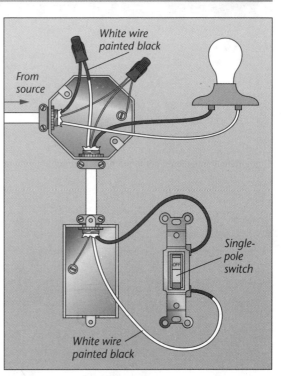

White wire painted black

From source

Single-pole switch

White wire painted black

Light at the end of the circuit

Use the following wiring diagrams to guide you when installing a replacement switch and in planning a circuit extension. In the example above, the circuit ends at a light fixture controlled by a single-pole pull-chain switch. In the example at right, a single-pole wall switch controls a light at the end of the circuit.

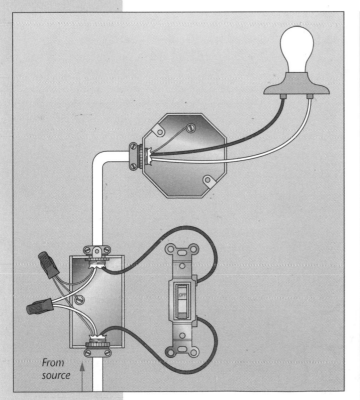

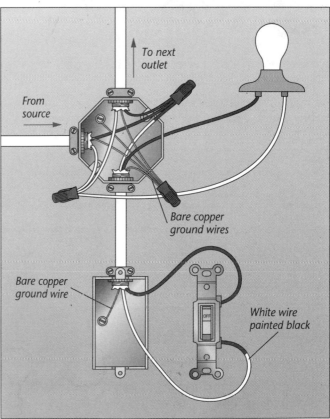

To next outlet

From source

Bare copper ground wires

Bare copper ground wire

White wire painted black

Switch in the middle of the circuit

In this wiring example, power goes through a single-pole switch that is located in the middle of a circuit (two or more cables enter the box). The switch controls a light at the end of the circuit.

Light in the middle of the circuit

In this example, the light is in the middle of a circuit (two or more cables enter the box), and the switch is wired in a switch loop. The switch controls the light in the middle of the circuit run.

Wiring three-way switches

Middle of the circuit

To wire a pair of three-way switches, run the hot wire from the source to the common terminal of one switch; run the hot wire from the light to the common terminal of the other switch. Then wire the four remaining terminals by running two hot wires between the two terminals on one switch and the two terminals on the other switch. In this example, the light in the middle of the circuit is controlled by a pair of three-way switches.

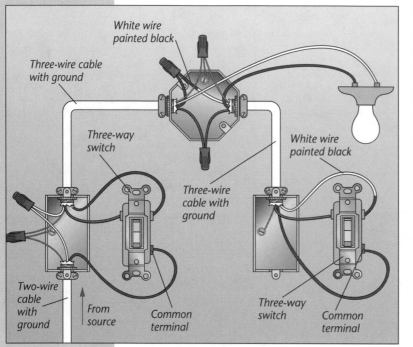

White wire painted black

Three-wire cable with ground

Three-way switch

White wire painted black

Three-wire cable with ground

White wire painted black

Two-wire cable with ground

From source

Common terminal

Three-way switch

Common terminal

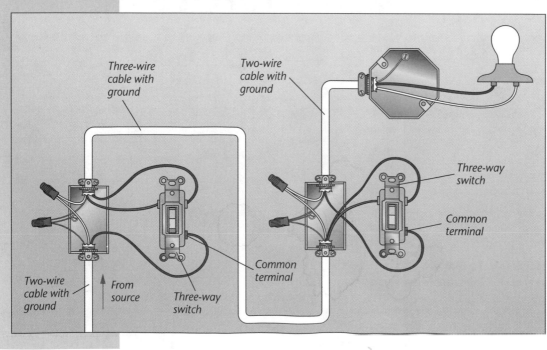

White wire painted black

From source

White wire painted black

Two-wire cable with ground

Three-wire cable with ground

White wires painted black

End of the circuit

A light is wired between a pair of three-way switches. CAUTION: Check the location of the common terminal on the switch (it will be marked); if it is different from this example, connect the black (hot) wire that runs between the switches to the common terminal on each switch.

Three-wire cable with ground

Two-wire cable with ground

Three-way switch

Common terminal

Two-wire cable with ground

From source

Three-way switch

Common terminal

End of the circuit

Power goes through a pair of three-way switches to a light at the end of the circuit. CAUTION: Check the location of the marked common terminal; if it is different from this example, connect the black (hot) wire that runs between the switches to the common terminal on each switch.

Installing a switch

TOOLKIT
- Cable ripper
- Wire stripper
- Diagonal-cutting pliers
- Screwdriver
- Long-nose pliers

1 ▶ Preparing the wires

Turn off power to the circuit at the service panel *(page 21)*. If you are installing a new switch, install the box *(page 70)*. Then, secure the cables to the box so that 6" to 8" of each cable extends into the box. Strip the outer sheath of insulation from the cables *(page 10)*, removing the sheath and all separation materials. Strip off 1/2" to 3/4" insulation from each wire *(right)*. If you are replacing a switch, unscrew the faceplate, pull the switch out of the box, then check to confirm that the circuit is dead *(page 8)*. Detach the wires from the old switch.

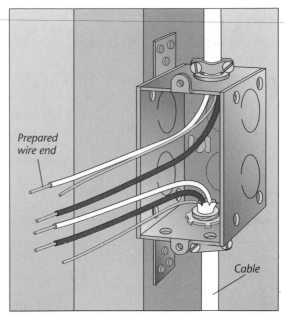

Prepared wire end

Cable

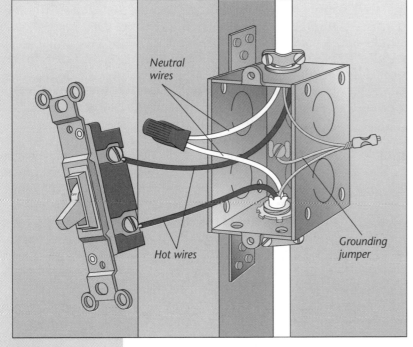

Neutral wires

Hot wires

Grounding jumper

2 ▶ Connecting the new switch

Join the two neutral (white) wires, and screw on a wire nut. Make a grounding connection by bonding the two grounding wires with a compression sleeve or wire nut. If the box is metal, also attach a grounding jumper to the grounding screw in the back of the box. Form the exposed wire ends of the two hot (black) wires into loops and secure them to the screw terminals on the switch. Tighten the screws to secure the connection *(left)*.

3 ▶ Securing the switch

Push the wires and the new switch into the box. Screw the mounting strap on the switch to the box; if necessary, adjust the screws in the mounting slots until the switch is straight. If the switch isn't flush with the wall surface, remove the plaster ears from the mounting strap and use them as shims to bring the switch forward. Screw on the faceplate *(right)*.

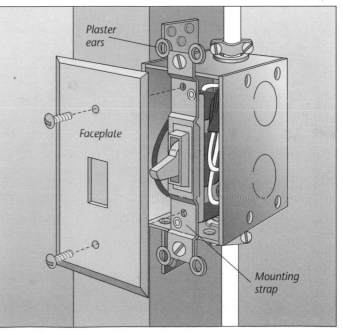

Plaster ears

Faceplate

Mounting strap

RECEPTACLE WIRING

Grounded receptacles consist of an upper and lower outlet with three slots. The larger (neutral) slot accepts the wide prong of a three-prong plug; the smaller (hot) slot is for the narrow prong, and the U-shaped grounding slot is for the grounding prong. The Code requires that all receptacles for 15- or 20-amp, 120-volt branch circuits (most of the circuits in your home) be of the grounding type shown below.

Screw terminals: Receptacles have three different colors of screw terminals. The brass-colored screws, on one side of the receptacle, are hot terminals; the white-or silver-colored screws, on the opposite side, are neutral terminals; and the green screw is the grounding terminal.

Backwired receptacles: If the receptacle is a backwired type, the black and white wires are inserted into the holes located on the back of the receptacle. Black wires are inserted into the holes located on the same side of the receptacle as the brass-colored screws; white wires are inserted into the holes located on the same side as the silver-colored screws. A wire gauge on the back shows how much insulation to strip off the wire ends. The grounding wire must still be attached to the green screw terminal on the receptacle.

Wiring requirements: Like switches, all receptacles are rated for a specific amperage and voltage. This information is stamped clearly on the front of the receptacle. Be sure you buy what you need.

240-volt receptacles: To eliminate the possibility of plugging a 120-volt appliance into a 240-volt receptacle, higher-voltage circuits use special receptacles and matching attachment plugs, shown opposite.

WIRING CONFIGURATIONS

Receptacles can be wired in a number of ways depending on the location of the receptacle in the circuit. If you are replacing an existing receptacle, you can determine the location of the receptacle by counting the number of cables entering the box (first remove the faceplate and pull the receptacle from the box). A receptacle with two or more cables entering the box is in the middle of the circuit (one cable brings power to the receptacle; the other cable sends power to the next box on the circuit). If there is one cable in the box, the receptacle is at the end of the circuit. Receptacle wiring also differs if the receptacle is controlled by a switch.

The diagrams on pages 49 and 50 show typical wiring configurations for receptacles in the middle of the circuit and at the end of the circuit. Use them as a reference when you are installing a receptacle. If you are replacing a defective receptacle, take note of its wiring configuration before you detach the wires.

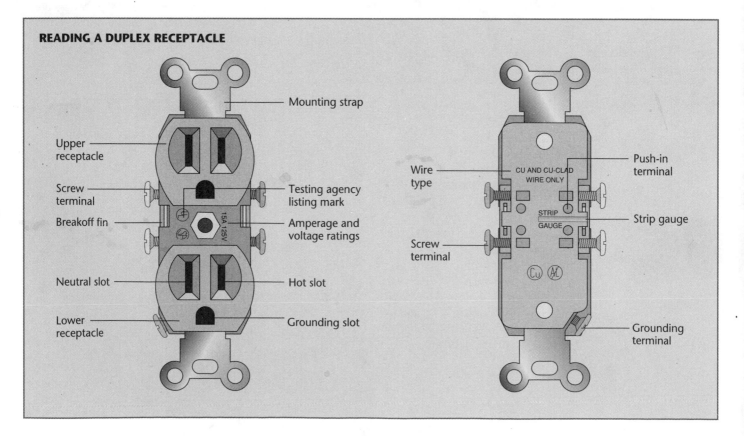

READING A DUPLEX RECEPTACLE

Mounting strap

Upper receptacle

Screw terminal

Breakoff fin

Testing agency listing mark

Amperage and voltage ratings

15A 125V

Neutral slot

Hot slot

Lower receptacle

Grounding slot

Wire type

CU AND CU-CLAD WIRE ONLY

Push-in terminal

STRIP GAUGE

Strip gauge

Screw terminal

Cu AL

Grounding terminal

SPECIAL RECEPTACLES AND GFCIS

Circuit breaker GFCI
The ground fault circuit interrupter (GFCI, or GFI) protects against electric shock. Whenever the amounts of incoming and outgoing current are not equal—indicating current leakage (a "ground fault")—the GFCI opens the circuit instantly, cutting off the power. GFCIs are built to trip in $\frac{1}{40}$ of a second in the event of a ground fault of 0.005 ampere. The GFCI breaker, shown at right, is installed in the service panel; it monitors the amount of current going to and coming from an entire circuit.

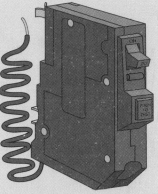

Receptacle GFCI
A GFCI receptacle monitors the flow of electricity to the receptacle, as well as all devices installed in the circuit from that point forward. The Code requires that receptacles in bathrooms, kitchens, garages, and other damp locations are protected by a circuit breaker GFCI. Another option is to install a receptacle GFCI in these locations.

Air conditioner receptacle
30 amps; 250 volts

Dryer receptacle
30 amps;
125/250 volts

Range receptacle
50 amps;
125/250 volts

Wiring a receptacle

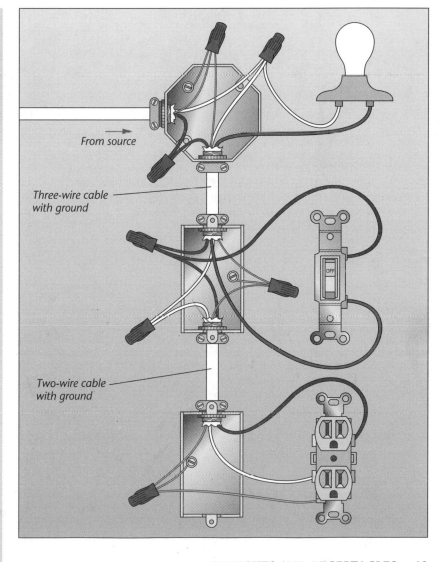

From source

Three-wire cable with ground

Two-wire cable with ground

Receptacle at the end of the circuit
In this example, a switch is wired ahead of the receptacle in the circuit (two cables enter the switch box). The switch controls a light. The receptacle is at the end of the circuit (one cable enters the box). Both the upper and lower outlets of the receptacle are always hot.

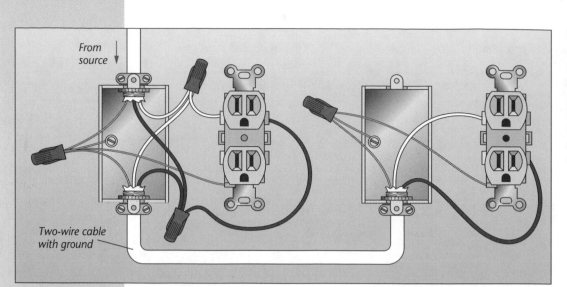

Receptacle at the end of the circuit
In this example, the receptacles are wired parallel to each other in the same circuit. Both the upper and lower outlets of each receptacle are always hot.

From source

Two-wire cable with ground

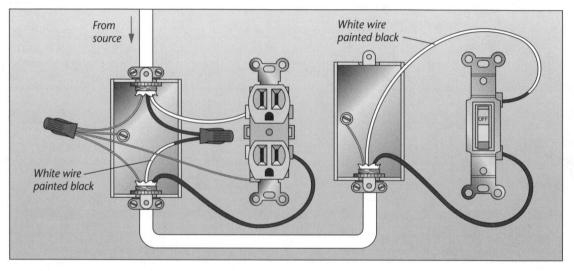

From source

White wire painted black

White wire painted black

Switch-controlled receptacle
Both the upper and lower outlets of this receptacle, located at the end of a circuit, are controlled by a single-pole switch. When the switch is in the ON position, the receptacle is hot; when the switch is turned off, the receptacle does not receive power.

Split-circuit receptacle
In this example, the metal tab connecting the upper and lower outlets has been removed *(page 52)* and the outlets operate independently. One outlet of this duplex receptacle is always hot, while the other half is controlled by a switch. When the switch is on, the outlet receives power.

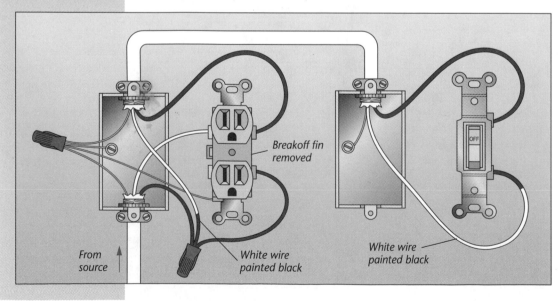

Breakoff fin removed

White wire painted black

White wire painted black

From source

INSTALLING RECEPTACLES

Many receptacles come with two sets of terminals: screw terminals and backwiring holes. If you are using screw terminals, attach the wires to the receptacle, as illustrated on page 47. Switches also can be backwired using the same technique.

To backwire a receptacle, make the wire-to-terminal connections by simply poking each wire end into a hole. To determine how much insulation to strip from each wire end, use the gauge that's molded into the back of the receptacle as a guide. Then, strip off the required insulation and poke the bare wire end into the appropriate hole. A jaw inside the hole allows the wire to enter, but prevents it being withdrawn unless you release the tension by inserting a small screwdriver blade into a special slot next to the hole. Backwiring is recommended for copper and copper-clad aluminum wires only—not for aluminum wires. When using the backwired terminals, tighten unused screw terminals.

Back-wiring a receptacle

TOOLKIT
• Diagonal-cutting pliers
• Wire strippers

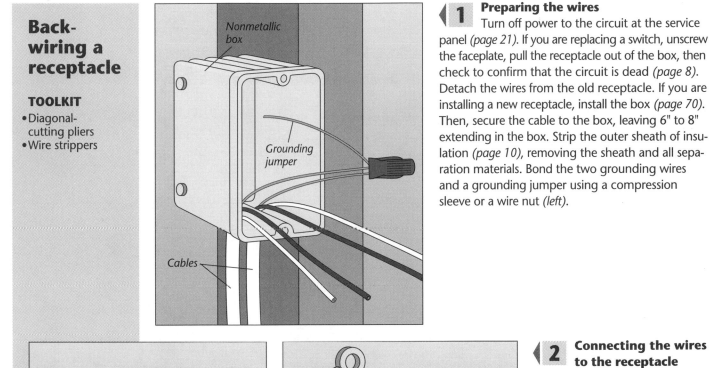

Nonmetallic box

Grounding jumper

Cables

1 Preparing the wires
Turn off power to the circuit at the service panel *(page 21)*. If you are replacing a switch, unscrew the faceplate, pull the receptacle out of the box, then check to confirm that the circuit is dead *(page 8)*. Detach the wires from the old receptacle. If you are installing a new receptacle, install the box *(page 70)*. Then, secure the cable to the box, leaving 6" to 8" extending in the box. Strip the outer sheath of insulation *(page 10)*, removing the sheath and all separation materials. Bond the two grounding wires and a grounding jumper using a compression sleeve or a wire nut *(left)*.

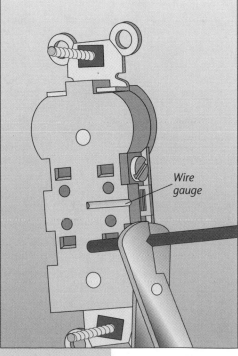

Wire gauge

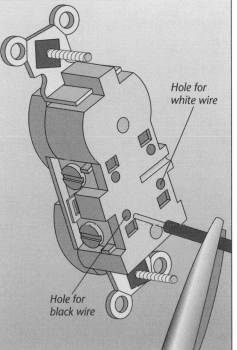

Hole for white wire

Hole for black wire

2 Connecting the wires to the receptacle
Using the molded gauge on the back of the receptacle, measure the amount of insulation to strip off the end of each wire, then use wire strippers to remove the insulation *(far left)*. Next, insert each wire into its proper hole on the back of the receptacle: The hot (black) wire goes into the hole on the same side of the receptacle as the brass screw terminals *(near left)* and the neutral (white) wire goes into the opposite hole. Attach the grounding jumper to the grounding screw on the receptacle, then tighten the unused screw terminals. Note: Backwiring is suitable for copper wire only.

3 ▶ Mounting the receptacle

Gently fold the wires into the box and set the receptacle in place. Screw the mounting strap to the box; if necessary, adjust the screws in the mounting slots until the receptacle is straight. If the receptacle isn't flush with the wall surface, use shims to bring it forward. Screw on the faceplate *(right)*.

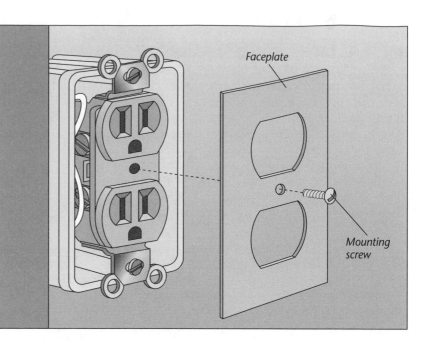

Faceplate

Mounting screw

SPLIT-CIRCUIT RECEPTACLES

Occasionally it may be appropriate to have the outlets of a duplex receptacle operate independently of each other. For example, you might want one outlet to be controlled by a switch and the other one to be always hot. Or you may wish to wire the two outlets of a receptacle into different circuits.

The wiring diagram on page 50 shows a receptacle wired so that one half is controlled by a switch (when the switch is turned on, the upper duplex receives power; when the switch is turned off, the upper duplex is dead); the lower duplex is always hot.

To make the outlets operate independently, use pliers or a screwdriver to remove the breakoff fin that connects them *(right)*.

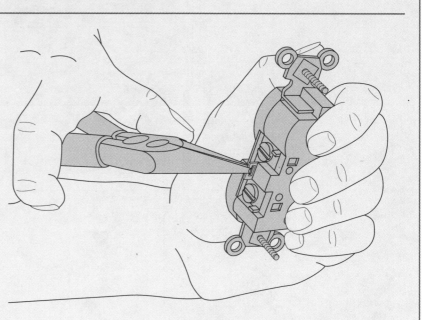

WIRING GROUNDED RECEPTACLES

All grounding-type receptacles must be grounded, whether they are installed as replacements in existing wiring or installed in new work. In new work, simply connect the receptacle to the circuit wires as shown on page 51. If you are replacing an ungrounded receptacle in an existing circuit that doesn't have a grounding wire in the cable, you must replace the receptacle with an ungrounded receptacle, a GFCI receptacle, or a grounding adapter plug *(below)*.

Unlike ungrounded receptacles, grounded receptacles have a green hexagonal screw terminal located near the lower U-shaped slot. The grounding wire from the cable or a grounding jumper wire must be attached to the green screw terminal on the receptacle.

Aluminum wiring: Receptacles marked CO-ALR can be used with either copper or aluminum wire. Unmarked receptacles and those marked CU-AL can be used with copper wire only. If you have aluminum wiring, use the screw terminals only.

Parallel wiring: A usual circuit arrangement is for several receptacles to be wired in parallel. Follow the wiring shown on page 50 when installing a receptacle in this type of circuit.

Grounding adapter plugs: Many portable appliances and tools have a grounding wire that eliminates the possibility of electric shock. A three-prong plug indicates the presence of a grounding wire. This wire connects to the circuit grounding wire through the third hole of a grounding-type receptacle. If your receptacles are the two-prong variety, you can use an adapter plug or change the receptacle, after checking that the receptacle box is grounded.

An adapter plug is effective only if the receptacle box is grounded and if you connect the screw lug properly, as shown below. If your circuit wiring runs in conduit or is armored cable or nonmetallic sheathed cable with ground, chances are that the box is grounded. Don't assume, however; test to be sure.

Installing a grounding-adapter plug

TOOLKIT
• Neon tester
• Screwdriver

Testing for grounding
Before installing a grounding-adapter plug, test to confirm that the receptacle box is grounded. With power to the circuit on, insert one probe of a neon tester into one slot in the receptacle as shown, and place the other probe on the mounting screw. Repeat the testing procedure with the other slot. If the tester lights up when the probe is in one slot of the receptacle, the box is grounded and you can install an adapter plug.

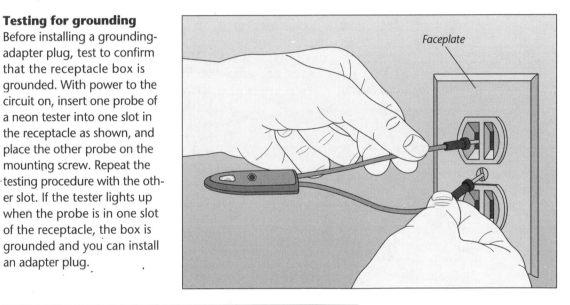

Faceplate

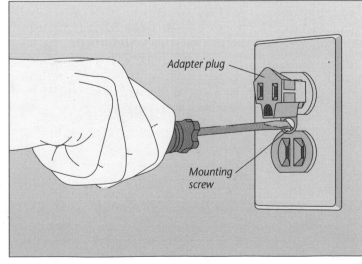

Adapter plug

Mounting screw

Installing an adapter plug
Loosen the mounting screw on the faceplate of the receptacle. Plug the adapter into one of the outlets on the receptacle, and fit the screw lug attached to the adapter plug under the faceplate mounting screw. Tighten the screw to secure the connection *(left)*.

ADDING AND EXTENDING CIRCUITS

This chapter provides specific techniques for installing concealed wiring in homes where wall, ceiling, and floor coverings are already in place. It also offers advice for routing cable in new homes before the walls, ceilings, and floors have been installed.

Before beginning any work, read through this chapter to get a feel for the project ahead. Then check with your local building department about getting an electrical permit. Obtaining a permit and requesting inspection add up to a solid guarantee that the work is performed properly. It's also an inexpensive way to get expert advice from a professional—your electrical inspector.

Although routing cable is not difficult, it can be a time-consuming task. A fish tape, shown on page 5, helps route cable from box opening to box opening. Once the cable has been fed to the new box locations, the boxes for switches, receptacles, and light fixtures are installed and the devices are connected to the circuit wiring. This chapter explains how to use the hot wire in an existing box as the power source. However, if you are installing new wiring, seek the advice of an electrical inspector or have a qualified electrician make the connections at the service panel.

The techniques for routing wire within walls apply only to wood frame homes; for houses with masonry walls or floors, consider installing surface wiring *(page 61)*.

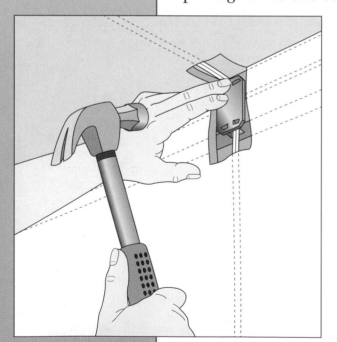

Cable installed less than 1¹/₄ inches from the surface of a wood member, such as a stud or joist, must be protected by a ¹/₁₆-inch metal plate.

There are three things that can be done to upgrade your existing electrical system: extend an existing circuit, add a new circuit, or install a subpanel. Remember: The number of receptacles, circuits, or subpanels is not important. What is important is the total house load; it must not exceed the total service rating for the house (page 28).

Extending a circuit: One of the key requirements for tapping into an existing circuit is the presence of both a hot and a neutral wire that are in direct connection with the source at the service panel. This means that any switch, receptacle or light fixture located in the middle or at the end of a circuit can be used.

One exception is a switch box that is wired with two hot wires only, as in the case of a switch loop (page 44). Note: When tapping into a circuit at a switch, it is important to identify the hot wire that leads from the source. If a circuit extension is wired inadvertently into the hot wire, the switch will control the extension. When the switch is in the off position, any devices beyond the switch will not receive power.

The illustration on page 49 shows how to extend a circuit from a receptacle and a switch. Note that the hot wire going to the receptacle is connected to the hot wire from the source. Circuits also can be extended from a switch (page 45).

There are a few more requirements: The wires must meet in a box, and the box must be large enough to accommodate the three wires of the new cable. Table IV on page 7 provides the Code requirements for the allowable number of conductors per box. If necessary, remove the old box and install a larger one.

Be sure to use the same size wire for the extension as the existing circuit wires (assuming the existing circuit wires are the correct size). The box must also have a knockout through which the new cable can be inserted and the cable must be supported by an interior or exterior clamp as it enters the box.

Access is very important, too. If there is a good, accessible power source in an existing box, but the box is too small to accommodate another cable, consider exchanging the box for a larger one.

Adding a new circuit: Adding a new circuit is often the answer when an existing circuit can't handle a new load or when a new appliance requires its own circuit. Before adding a new circuit, though, calculate the total house load including the new load to make sure it will still be within your service rating. Note that all new 120-volt branch circuits must have a grounding wire and must comply with present code requirements (consult "Branch circuit requirements" on page 56).

Adding a subpanel: The installation of a subpanel avoids long circuit runs and is also a convenient way to add new circuits. Installing a subpanel is beyond the scope of this book. You will have to consult an electrician to have one installed.

ASK A PRO

PLANNING A NEW CIRCUIT

The first step in planning a new circuit is to draw a diagram showing the location of each proposed switch, receptacle, light fixture, and major appliance. Refer back to the symbols shown in "Circuit mapping" on page 27 to make this easier. The next step is to design the circuit. When doing this, keep in mind that it is unwise to have a single circuit supplying the lights for an entire section or floor of a house. Try to plan each circuit so one area of the home won't be left in the dark in the event that the circuit fails.

Circuits fall into three categories: 120-volt, 120/240-volt, and 240-volt circuits. Most circuits in the home are 120-volt circuits. Some appliances, however, such as an electric range, or clothes dryer, require inputs of both 120 and 240 volts. Timing devices and motors in these appliances need 120 volts, and heating elements need the additional power of 240 volts. Electric water heaters and central air conditioners are examples of appliances that require a dedicated 240-volt circuit. Older homes with a two-wire service entrance of less

than 100 amps can't support many modern electrical appliances. To add a large load such as a range or dryer, the service from the utility company must be increased to three-wire at 100 amps or more. If you are confused by the load calculations and are unsure whether you can add a new load, prepare a list of all your major appliances and their nameplate ratings, the square footage of your home, and the type of service you want. Then, consult your local electrical inspector who can tell you what is the best service to meet your requirements.

The actual connection of circuits in the service panel is usually done once all the new circuits have been run. You will need the services of a qualified electrician to connect the circuits at the service panel, and to install any required individual disconnects. (Some stationary, motor-operated appliances, such as a garbage disposal, the motor of a gas heater, or a central air conditioner, require a separate fuse block or circuit breaker at the service panel.)

PLANNING NEW WIRING ROUTES

Planning is the crucial first step in putting in a wiring system from scratch. The time you spend at this stage can save both time and money when you do the actual wiring.

Branch circuit requirements: Start your planning by reviewing the following *National Electrical Code* branch circuit requirements. Remember that these are minimum requirements; more circuits can (and, in many cases, should) be added.

Kitchen and related areas: The areas of a home most restricted by the Code include the kitchen, pantry, dining room, family room, and breakfast room. The receptacles in these areas must be served by at least two 20-amp small appliance circuits. These receptacles are intended for small appliances, such as those used in food preparation and refrigeration. No light fixtures or other outlets can be connected to these circuits.

The receptacles should be evenly distributed between the small appliance circuits. That is, if there are two small appliance circuits and eight receptacles required to serve the kitchen, four receptacles should be on one circuit and four on the other.

If the kitchen will have a dishwasher and/or garbage disposal unit, you must provide a separate 20-amp cir-cuit for each of these appliances. An electric range should be supplied by an individual 50-amp, 120/240-volt major appliance circuit.

Laundry area: The Code requires a separate 20-amp circuit to supply the receptacle for a washing machine. If the laundry equipment will also include an electric dryer, you will need an individual 30-amp, 120/240-volt major appliance circuit for it.

The rest of the house: Circuit requirements for the living room, bedrooms, and bathroom are not as specific as they are for the previously mentioned areas of a house. In fact, once you've assigned the circuits for the restricted areas, the rest of the circuits can be 15-amp general purpose circuits. These circuits are used to supply light fixtures, switches, and receptacles with power. (Note: This excludes other major appliance circuits, such as those needed for a water heater or a central heating system.)

By dividing 500 square feet into the total square footage of your home, you can find out how many 15-amp general purpose circuits you should have. If your home is 1,500 square feet (based on outside measurements), you should allow at least three 15-amp circuits. If you have 1,600 square feet, allow at least four.

REQUIRED RECEPTACLES AND LIGHTING FIXTURES

Specific receptacle and lighting fixture requirements:

Receptacles: For most areas of a house, the required number of receptacles depends on the size of each room. Any wall space two feet or more in width must have a receptacle. Receptacles must be spaced not more than 12 feet apart and not more than six feet from each door or opening (this includes archways but not windows). This would allow a lamp or appliance with a six-foot cord to be used near any wall without an extension cord.

When a receptacle is located behind a stationary appliance such as a refrigerator, it is not considered as one of those required every 12 feet.

In the kitchen and eating areas, every counter space wider than 12 inches should have a receptacle. Every basement is required to have at least one receptacle.

GFCIs: At least one receptacle is also required near the water basin in a bathroom, on the outside of the house, and in the garage. These areas require special treatment, however, because of the possibility that you might contact a grounded metal plumbing fixture or a concrete patio floor at the same time you are using a defective electri-cal appliance. For this reason, bathroom, outdoor, and garage receptacles must be protected by ground fault circuit interrupters (GFCIs).

The Code permits the installation of GFCI protection in either of two ways. You can use a receptacle with a GFCI built right into it, or you can install a GFCI in the service panel in place of the circuit breaker protecting that particular circuit. For more information about GFCIs, see page 49.

Lighting fixtures: Required lighting fixtures fall into two groups: those that must be controlled by a wall switch, and those that can have any kind of turn-on arrangement.

The Code states that every room, hallway, stairway, attached garage, and outdoor entrance must have at least one lighting fixture controlled by a wall switch. However, in rooms other than kitchens and bathrooms, the wall switch can control one or more receptacles (which lamps can be plugged into) rather than an actual lighting fixture such as a ceiling or wall-mounted light.

In the "any kind of switching" category, the Code requires one lighting fixture in a utility room, attic, basement, and underfloor space where used for storage or containing equipment that may require servicing.

ACCESS FOR CABLE

Wood frame homes are not all built the same way, but most have 2x4 stud walls, 2x8 (or larger) floor joists, and 2x6 (or larger) ceiling joists. These wooden structural members are normally spaced 16 inches apart from center to center. In some new homes, however, the spacing is 24 inches, and in some roughly built older homes it's somewhat random. The illustration below shows the skeleton of a typical wood frame house.

In new construction, all basic wiring is done before wall, ceiling, and floor coverings are added. Extending a circuit in a finished house, however, is a different story. You have to find ways to route cable behind existing walls, above ceilings, and under floors *(page 60)*.

Familiarize yourself with your home's construction so that you can select the most direct route from the power source to the locations for new devices. The best route for a cable run is one that is direct and accessible. Accessibility is generally more important than directness. The savings in time and effort from avoiding extensive cutting and patching of walls, ceilings, and floors nearly always offsets the added material costs for an indirect cable run.

Where you have access: In some parts of your home, installing cable and boxes might be quite easy. These are areas such as attic floors and unfinished basement ceilings where wall, ceiling, and floor coverings are attached only to one side of the framing. You simply work from the uncovered side, drilling holes and threading cable through studs or joists. You can also "fish" cable through finished walls from these locations *(page 60)*. When in an attic, don't put any weight on the ceiling material between joists. Step only on the joists, or put planks across them for more ease; be sure to walk gently so you don't crack the ceiling surface.

Where access is limited: Getting cables into walls, floors, or ceilings that have coverings on both sides involves cutting through the coverings, installing cable, and patching up the holes. The amount and difficulty of cutting and patching depends only partly on where the cable goes; it's also determined by the surface material.

The most common wall and ceiling covering, gypsum wallboard, is relatively easy to cut away and replace. But some other materials, such as ceramic tile, some types of wood flooring, and plaster, are more difficult to cut and patch and should be left alone when possible.

A TYPICAL WOOD FRAME HOUSE

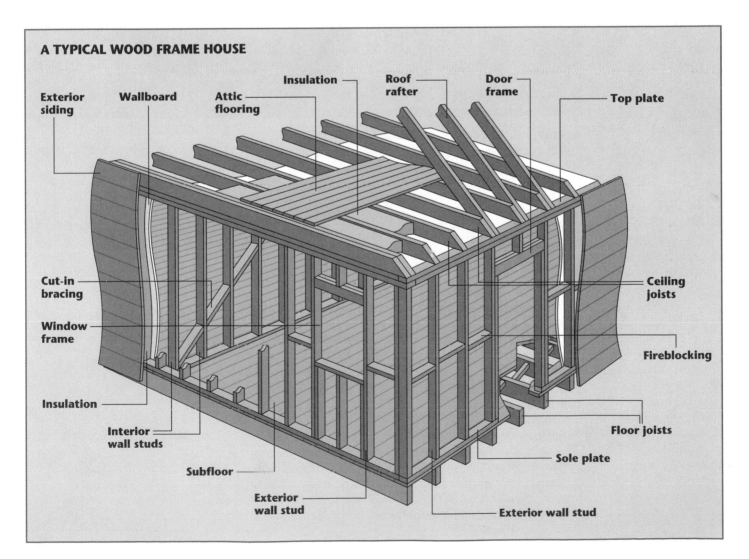

Exterior siding · Wallboard · Attic flooring · Insulation · Roof rafter · Door frame · Top plate · Cut-in bracing · Window frame · Insulation · Interior wall studs · Subfloor · Exterior wall stud · Ceiling joists · Fireblocking · Floor joists · Sole plate · Exterior wall stud

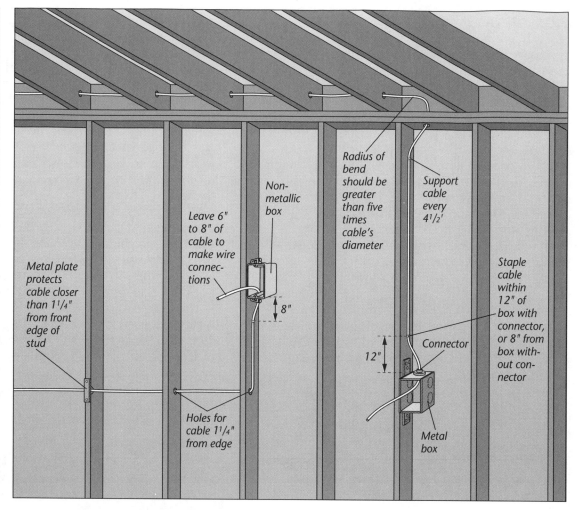

Radius of
bend
should be
greater
than five
times
cable's
diameter

Non-
metallic
box

Support
cable
every
4¹/₂'

Staple
cable
within
12" of
box with
connector,
or 8" from
box with-
out con-
nector

Leave 6"
to 8" of
cable to
make wire
connec-
tions

8"

Metal plate
protects
cable closer
than 1¹/₄"
from front
edge of
stud

12"

Connector

Holes for
cable 1¹/₄"
from edge

Metal
box

Routing cable in walls and ceilings

This illustration shows a typical route for running cable through walls and ceilings. To avoid nailing through the cable once the walls and ceilings are installed, run the cable through the studs and joists. Drill holes for cable 1¹/₄" from the edge of wall studs; drill holes through the center of the joists to route the cable from joist to joist.

ASK A PRO

WHAT'S THE BEST WAY TO ATTACH CABLE?

In exposed (new) wiring, cable must be stapled or supported with straps every 4¹/₂ feet and within 12 inches of each metal box and eight inches of each nonmetallic box. When using cable staples and clamps (right), be careful that you don't staple through or smash the cable. Use metal plates to protect cable that is installed closer than 1¹/₄ inches from the front edge of a stud or other structural member. Cable staples or supports are not required when cable is fished behind walls, floors, or ceilings in concealed (old) work. However, the cable must be clamped to boxes using built-in cable clamps, metal cable connectors or plastic cable connectors (if the box is nonmetallic). There is one exception: NM cable need not be clamped to a nonmetallic box if it is stapled within eight inches of the box.

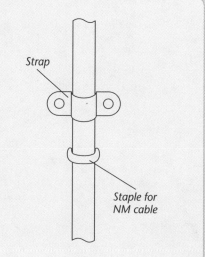

Strap

Staple for
NM cable

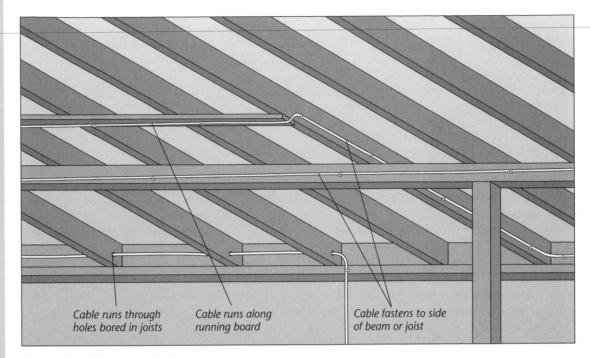

Cable runs through
holes bored in joists

Cable runs along
running board

Cable fastens to side
of beam or joist

Running cable through the basement

When running cable under the floor at an angle to floor joists, NM cable with two conductors in sizes smaller than #6, or with three conductors in sizes smaller than #8, must be routed through the joists, secured to a running board, or supported on the side surface of structural members. Larger NM cable may be stapled directly to the bottom edges of the joists.

Running cable in the attic

Accessibility dictates how cable runs in an attic. If a permanent staircase or ladder leads to the attic, cable running at an angle to the joists must be protected by guard strips. In an attic reached through a crawl hole with no permanent stairs or ladder, the cable must be protected by guard strips only within 6' of the hole *(left)*. Beyond 6', cable may lie on top of the ceiling joists.

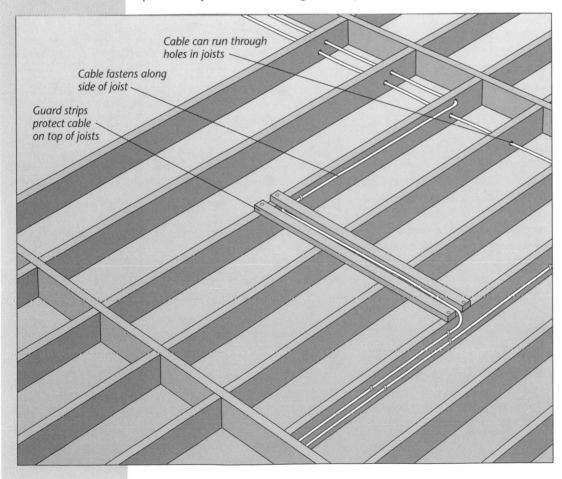

Cable can run through
holes in joists

Cable fastens along
side of joist

Guard strips
protect cable
on top of joists

PLANNING A CIRCUIT EXTENSION

Before routing cable, you must select the existing box that will provide power to the extension, as well as the locations for the new devices. Always disconnect power to the circuit you will be working on *(page 21)*. Then, purchase the right cable *(page 66)* and boxes *(page 68)* for the job. Fish tapes feed cable over long runs; for short distances, use a straightened coat hanger or a length of stiff wire with one end bent into a hook. You may need to do some minor repairs to walls, ceilings, and floors once the wiring is completed.

Fishing cable for a short run with access

TOOLKIT
- Keyhole or saber saw
- Electric drill
- ³/₁₆" drill bit
- ³/₄" spade bit
- 2 fish tapes
- Cable strippers

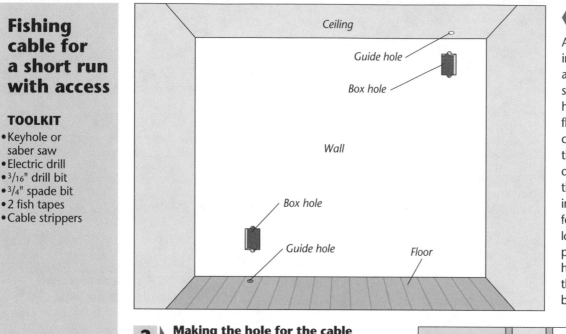

1 ▸ Making the first guide hole
After locating and making a hole for the box in an open space between studs, drill a small guide hole down through the floor or up through the ceiling to mark this location *(left)*. Using a ³/₁₆" drill bit, drill a hole through the floor or ceiling directly above the hole for the box. To find the location of the guide hole, poke a stiff wire into the hole so that the end of the wire is visible in the basement or attic.

2 ▸ Making the hole for the cable
Using a ³/₄" spade bit, drill next to your guide hole up through the sole plate from the basement or down through the top plates from the attic. As a rule of thumb, position the hole for the cable approximately 2" in from the location hole. Drill until you hit open space *(right)*; you may have to use an extension bit. Working in the basement or in the attic, run a fish tape through the hole for the cable. Feed the fish tape down the inside of the wall. Open the hooked end on another fish tape and feed it through the box hole, wiggling it around until it snags the hook on the first fish tape.

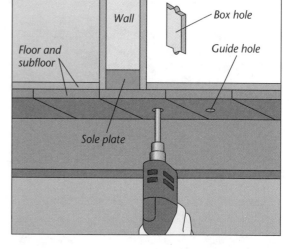

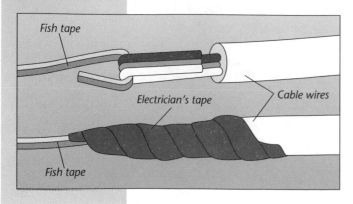

3 ▸ Fishing the cable
At the box hole, gently tug both fish tapes through the hole, and disconnect them. Measure and prepare the cable, stripping off approximately 8" of sheathing. Attach the cable to the end of the fish tape and wrap the connection with electrician's tape *(left)*. Draw the cable into the box hole. Working in the basement or in the attic, tug on the fish tape and cable. Run the cable along an exposed basement or attic joist, securing it with staples or straps. Attach the new cable to a power source.

Fishing cable for a long run with access

TOOLKIT
- Keyhole or saber saw
- Electric drill
- 3/16" drill bit
- 3/4" spade bit
- 2 fish tapes

1 ▶ Feeding the fish tape

Locate and make a hole for the box in open space between studs; then drill a 3/16" guide hole through the floor or up through the ceiling. Using a 3/4" spade bit, drill next to the guide hole up through the sole plate from the basement or down through the top plates from the attic. Working in the basement or in the attic, run a fish tape through the hole for the cable. Feed the fish tape down the inside of the wall. Open the hooked end on another fish tape and feed it through the box hole, wiggling it around until it snags the hook on the first fish tape *(right)*.

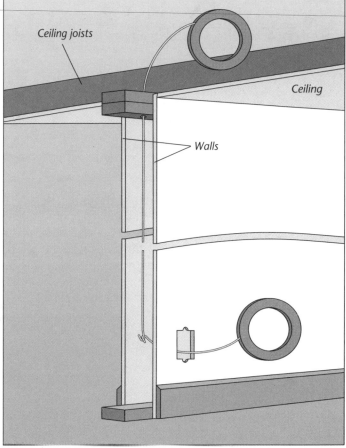

Ceiling joists

Walls

Ceiling

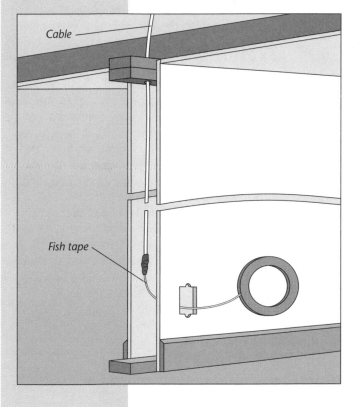

Cable

Fish tape

◀ 2 Feeding the cable

At the box hole, gently tug both fish tapes through the hole, and disconnect them. Measure and prepare the cable, stripping off approximately 8" of sheathing. Attach the cable to the end of the fish tape, securing it with electrician's tape. Begin drawing the cable into the box hole *(left)*. Working in the basement or in the attic, gently tug on the fish tape and the attached cable. Pulling slowly, work it through the wall to the box opening. You will have to attach the new cable to a power source.

QUICK FIX

WHAT'S THE QUICKEST WAY TO EXTEND A CIRCUIT?

Where routing wire through walls and when cutting into walls, ceilings, and floors is too difficult, surface wiring is the best answer. Safe and neat, surface wiring systems usually consist of protective channels (below) or strips that allow you to mount wiring and boxes on practically *any surface. Cable is fished through the channels; wall boxes also are surface mounted. Because surface wiring materials from various manufacturers differ somewhat, consult your electrical supplies dealer for more information about the various systems available.*

Routing cable behind a baseboard

TOOLKIT
- Pry bar
- Keyhole or saber saw
- Electric drill
- Chisel or utility knife
- Fish tape
- Hammer

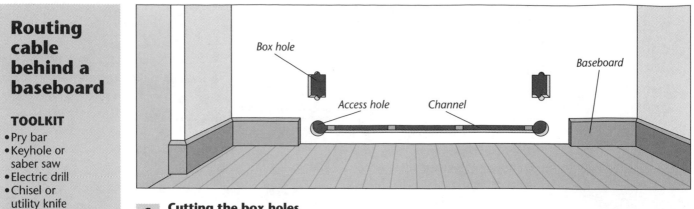

Box hole

Access hole   Channel

Baseboard

1 Cutting the box holes
If you are extending an existing circuit, de-energize the circuit you will be working on *(page 21)*. Mark the location for the new boxes and cut their holes *(page 70)*. Using a utility bar, gently pry off the baseboard between the box locations. In order to fish the cable from the box hole, drill an access hole for the cable through the wall. Locate each access hole so that it will be concealed when the baseboard is reinstalled. Using a chisel or utility knife, cut a channel in the wall to connect the two access holes *(above)*. Be sure to position the channel so that it will be concealed by the baseboard.

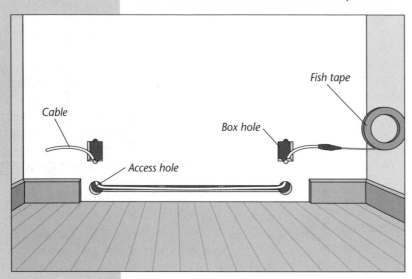

Cable

Box hole

Fish tape

Access hole

2 Fishing the cable
Feed a fish tape through one box hole, then pull it out the access hole directly below the box hole. Run the fish tape along the channel, feeding it through the other access hole and out of the second box hole. Measure and cut the required length of cable. Strip 8" of sheathing from one end of the cable. Pry open the hook at the end of the fish tape and attach the cable wires to the fish tape *(page 60)*. Gently pull on the fish tape, feeding the cable from box hole to box hole. Leave approximately 8" of cable extending from the first box *(left)*. Install metal plates to secure the cable to any studs *(below)*. You will have to attach the new cable to a power source. Reinstall the baseboard, taking care not to nail through the cable.

WORKING WITH MOLDING

When routing cable behind window or door molding, keep these points in mind:

1. Molding may split, so be sure you can buy replacement pieces before you begin.

2. Use a utility knife or a putty knife to break the paint bond between the molding and the wall or ceiling covering.

3. Use a 4" (or wider) putty knife or chisel to pry molding from the wall. Take your time, gently prying up the molding without cracking it.

4. Cable installed less than 1¹/₄" from a finished surface must be protected by a ¹/₁₆" metal plate *(right)* or run through thinwall conduit.

5. When nailing molding back up, position the nails above and below the channel in the wall so that you do not nail through the cable.

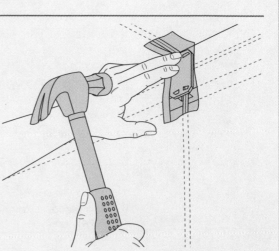

Routing cable behind a wall

TOOLKIT
- Keyhole or saber saw
- Chisel or utility knife
- Electric drill
- 3/4" spade bit

Routing cable through wall studs

Use a chisel or utility knife to cut a channel in the wall between box holes; center the ends of the channel over a stud. Using a 3/4" spade bit, drill through the center of each stud. Feed one end of the cable through a box hole, then run it through the studs to the second box hole.

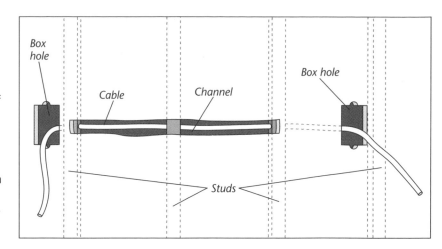

Routing cable around a doorway

TOOLKIT
- Keyhole or saber saw
- Putty knife
- Chisel or utility knife (optional)
- Prybar
- Hammer

Running cable behind a door frame

De-energize the circuit you will be working on *(page 21)*. Using a putty knife or chisel, gently pry up the molding around the door frame; also remove as much baseboard as necessary on either side of the door. Run the cable from an existing wall box to the doorway, routing the cable in a channel cut in the wall behind the baseboard. If this is not possible, you will have to route the cable behind the wall *(page 60)*. Route the cable around the doorway to the new box location, positioning the cable between the jamb and the frame. If necessary, use a chisel to notch any door frame spacers so that the cable fits flush. Attach the new cable to a power source *(page 76)*. Reinstall the door frame molding and any baseboard, taking care not to pierce the cable.

Installing back-to-back devices

TOOLKIT
- Keyhole or saber saw
- Screwdriver

Running cable between two boxes on opposite sides of a wall

De-energize the circuit you will be working on *(page 21)*. Mark the location for the new box, aligning it with the box on the other side of the wall, and cut its hole *(page 70)*. Unscrew the faceplate, pull the device that is to be the power source out of its box, and pry out a knockout from the back of the box. Measure and cut the required length of cable. You will also need a connector to secure the cable to the box. Insert the cable with its connector through the new box hole, feeding it into the source box. Connect the new device to the power source *(page 76)*.

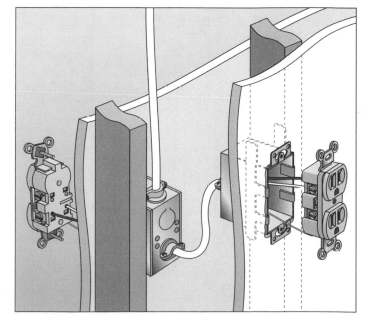

Adding a light and a switch

TOOLKIT
- Keyhole or saber saw
- Prybar
- Electric drill
- Chisel
- Fish tape
- Cable ripper
- Diagonal-cutting pliers
- Wire strippers
- Hammer

1 ▶ Making the box holes

De-energize the circuit you will be working on *(page 21)*. Mark the location for the fixture box between two ceiling joists and cut its hole *(page 70)*. Cut a hole for the switch box, and make a hole where the wall meets the ceiling. (Unless you want to run the cable through notched wall studs or behind molding to another switch location, plan to locate the switch directly below the ceiling hole.) Using a prybar, gently pry off the baseboard between the switch box location and the existing power source. In order to fish the cable from the box hole, you will need to drill an access hole for the cable through the wall, and chisel a channel in the wall *(page 63)*.

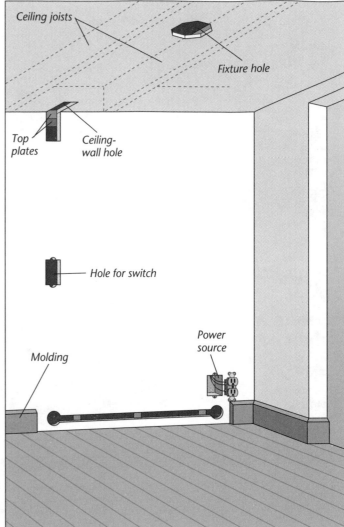

Ceiling joists

Fixture hole

Top plates

Ceiling-wall hole

Hole for switch

Power source

Molding

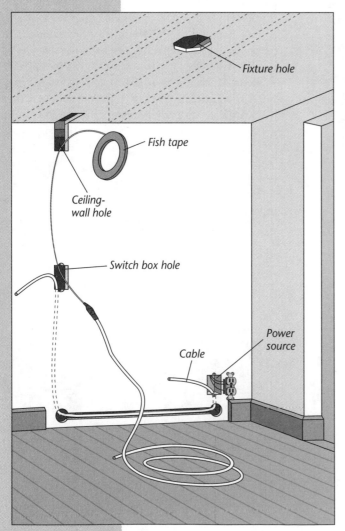

Fixture hole

Fish tape

Ceiling-wall hole

Switch box hole

Cable

Power source

◀ 2 Fishing the cable up the wall

Measure and cut the required length of cable to run between the power source box and the switch box hole. Begin fishing the cable by running it from the power source box to the switch box, feeding it along the channel in the wall behind the baseboard; leave about 1' of cable protruding from the switch box hole. Next, feed a fish tape down from the hole at the ceiling and wall seam, pulling the end of the fish tape through the switch box hole. Measure and cut the required length of cable to run between the fixture box hole and the switch box hole. Open the hook on the end of the fish tape and connect one end of the cable to it, securing it with electrician's tape. Gently pull on the fish tape, routing the cable up and out the ceiling-wall hole *(left)*.

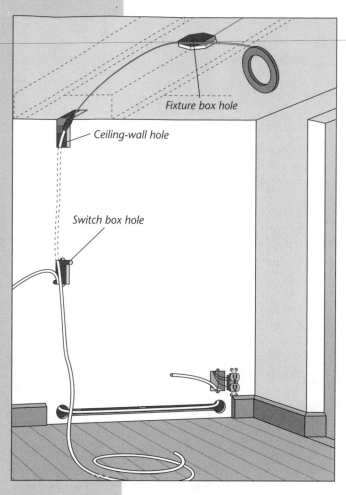

Fixture box hole

Ceiling-wall hole

Switch box hole

3 ▶ Fishing the cable to the fixture box hole

Disconnect the cable from the fish tape. Working at the fixture box hole, feed the fish tape through the fixture hole until it protrudes from the ceiling-wall hole. Open the hook on the end of the fish tape and connect one end of the cable to it, securing it with electrician's tape. Pull on the fish tape, routing the cable up and out the fixture box hole *(left)*.

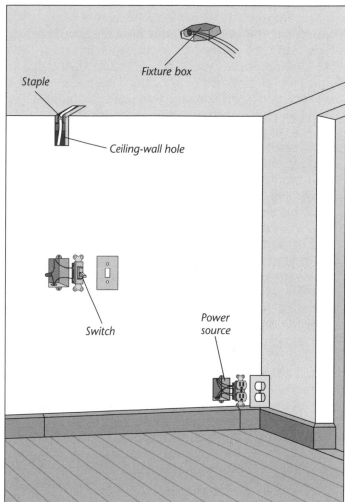

Fixture box

Staple

Ceiling-wall hole

Switch

Power source

4 ▶ Installing the switch and light

Working at the ceiling-wall hole, use a chisel to notch the top plates, then fit the cable into the notch so that it is recessed. Staple cable in place. Connect the cables to boxes, then mount the boxes to the wall and the ceiling. Prepare the wire ends of the cables, and make the wire connections to the fixture, the switch, and the power source. Patch any holes in the walls *(page 77)*, and reinstall the baseboard.

ASK A PRO

WHAT'S THE EASIEST WAY TO RUN CABLE ACROSS A CEILING?

When routing cable across a ceiling, try to run the cable parallel with the ceiling joists, not through them. To do this, begin by establishing which way the joists run across the ceiling. Working from a ladder, knock on the ceiling, listening for a solid sound, which indicates a ceiling joist. (A hollow sound reflects the empty space between the joists.) Ceiling joists normally are installed 16 inches on center.

ROUTING CABLE

Nonmetallic sheathed cable (NM), conduit, armored cable, and knob-and-tube (not approved for new installations, but may be used as an extension of existing wiring) represent four basic methods for wiring branch circuits. Today, nonmetallic sheathed cable is used in most residential wiring and is what we will be using throughout this chapter. This cable is a good example of a successful marriage of modern materials and technology. Nonmetallic sheathed cable comes in types NM (nonmetallic) and UF (underground feeder). Type AC metal-clad cable, although more expensive then NM cable, is sometimes used in residential wiring. Techniques for cutting and connecting Type AC metal-clad cable are shown on the opposite page.

How and where to run nonmetallic sheathed cable: Plan the circuit routes behind walls, below floors, and above ceilings. Make the routes as direct as possible, following structural building members wherever you can. Don't route cables where you're likely to accidentally nail through them later.

One option for a branch circuit is to run a 240-volt, three-wire circuit to a junction box and branch off from there into two 120-volt, two-wire runs for receptacles and/or light fixtures. Referred to as split-circuit or multiwire wiring, this use of a 240-volt circuit allows you to run the equivalent of two 10-volt branch circuits with less material and time.

After cutting holes but before mounting the boxes, you must run cable from the power source to the new box locations. Staple one end of the cable next to the source, leaving about a foot more than you think you'll need for the connection, then route the cable. Wait until you have all the new boxes wired and mounted before you make the actual hookup to the source.

If you're installing a new receptacle back-to-back to an existing one, routing cable is no problem. But under any other condition, this step will involve some patient work. Your goal here, as with routing cable in new construction, is to staple the cable to studs, joists, rafters, and other structural members where the cable parallels them and to pass the cable through holes where it runs at an angle or perpendicular to them.

Where you have access from below or above (for example, in a basement with an unfinished ceiling or an attic with no floor covering), it's easy to run cable along joists or through holes bored through them. From these locations you can fish cable through walls that are covered on both sides. From a basement you can generally fish cable up to a receptacle with little trouble. Working from an unfinished attic, running cable from switches to light fixtures is usually a simple job. Use the illustrations on pages 60 to 65 to guide you.

WORKING WITH NM CABLE

Estimating the length of cable: Begin by making a rough sketch of your cable route, including critical dimensions such as height of boxes from the floor and the distance between boxes. Add together all the dimensions. Then, for box-to-box runs, add 4 feet of extra cable (2 feet for each box) for mistakes, box connections, and unforeseen obstacles. When the cable goes directly from a panel (either the service panel or a subpanel), add 6 feet (4 for the panel and 2 feet for the box).

Drilling holes: When boring through joists or studs, use a relatively small drill bit—7/8 inch—to allow one or two runs of cable to be pulled through without too much struggle. An inexpensive spade bit or a long twist bit will both do the job. Try to drill in the center of the board, but if you end up less than 1 1/4 inches from the edge, you will have to tack a metal plate or a piece of 16-gauge metal over the edge to protect the cable from accidental damage.

Routing cable: Try to not kink or twist NM or UF cable during installation. You'll need some specialized tools to route the cable. Fish tapes (page 5) are the right tools to use for long cable runs. For shorter distances, you can improvise with straightened coat hangers or lengths of #12 wire with one end bent into a tight, blunt hook. (Be sure that whatever tool you use is long enough to span the entire distance plus an additional 2 feet.)

Fishing: You'll need an open space to fish through. The illustrations on page 60 show how to fish a short run where you have access from above or below. You also can route cable behind a baseboard (page 62), behind a wall (page 63), and around a doorway (page 63), and to a light and switch (page 64).

If you're going to attempt fishing more than a few feet, you'll need to work with a partner. Start by following steps 1 and 2 on page 60. Then, to make sure your passage is clear, have someone shine a flashlight in the box hole while you peer into the drilled hole to see if the light beam is visible. If it isn't, a fire block (or something else) is in the way. For drilling through this obstruction, you'll need several extension shafts for the drill bit. Drill through the block or other obstruction, then look for the light again. If you still can't see the light beam, you will have to move to another location or cut away some of the wall covering and notch the fire block.

WORKING WITH ARMORED CABLE

Type AC metal-clad cable (also known as BX cable), is very expensive; as a result it is seldom used today for residential wiring. If you do use it, take care to learn how to use it correctly. See your local inspector.

Where it can be used: Type AC cable may be used for branch circuits and subfeeds of both exposed (new) and concealed (old) wiring in dry locations only. AC cable may be run in the air spaces of masonry block or tile walls if they are dry and above ground level. You cannot bury type AC cable in the earth or in concrete, but you can embed it in a plaster finish over a brick or other masonry wall.

How and where to run AC cable: Wherever possible, route your circuit so that the cable follows the surface of structural members. Where you must run the cable at an angle to the members, drill holes in the center of the boards. A metal plate must be tacked to any board where a hole is drilled less than 1½ inches from the edge. Though the metal armor of AC cable is flexible, sharp bends can be damaging. The bend radius should be at least five times the diameter of the cable.

Routing AC cable: When routing AC cable at an angle to floor joists, attach the cable directly to each joist. When routing in attics, treat AC cable like NM cable.

Grounding: A special bonding strip is attached to the inside of the metal armor of all AC cable. This bonding strip provides the grounding path for AC cable wiring. Because of this, a separate grounding wire is not necessary when the cable is connected to a metal box. A jumper is still required, however, between the grounding terminal of a receptacle and the metal box.

Working with armored cable

TOOLKIT
• Fine-toothed hacksaw

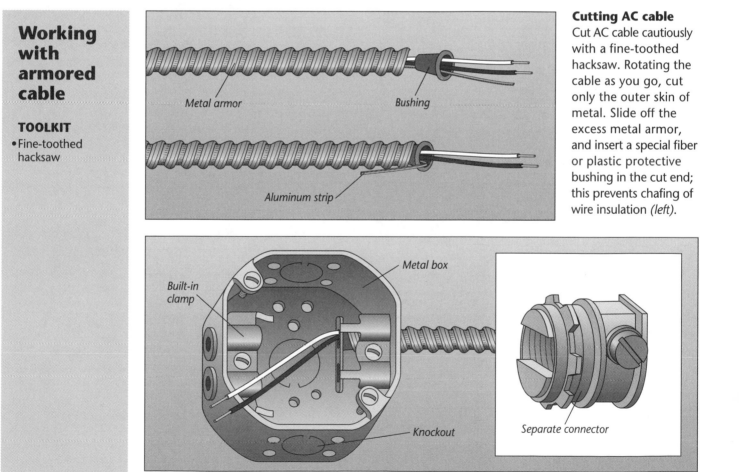

Metal armor

Bushing

Aluminum strip

Cutting AC cable
Cut AC cable cautiously with a fine-toothed hacksaw. Rotating the cable as you go, cut only the outer skin of metal. Slide off the excess metal armor, and insert a special fiber or plastic protective bushing in the cut end; this prevents chafing of wire insulation *(left)*.

Built-in clamp

Metal box

Knockout

Separate connector

Connecting AC cable to boxes
Use only staples or straps designed for use with AC cable. Type AC cable must be supported every 4½' and within 12" of each box. You can only use metal boxes when wiring with AC cable. At each termination, the cable must be secured to the box. Either use a separate connector *(inset)*, or use a box with built-in clamps especially designed for AC cable *(above)*. Both the connectors and cable clamps have slots so that the protective bushing is visible once the installation is completed.

ELECTRICAL BOXES

Before routing cable, you must choose and buy the right boxes, and cut holes in the wall or ceiling coverings for them. Boxes are connection points, either for joining wires or for connection to devices such as receptacles, switches, and fixtures. Regardless of general trade terminology, most boxes are interchangeable in function. For example, with appropriate contents and covers, the same box could be used as an outlet box, a junction box, or a switch box.

The variety of sizes and shapes corresponds to variations in wiring methods, kind and number of devices attached to the box, and number of wires entering it. Boxes come in both metal and nonmetallic versions. Metal is sturdier, but you must ground metal boxes. Nonmetallic boxes cost less and don't require grounding, but they are breakable. When mounting one with nails, be careful to hammer only the nails, not the box. Each box has a certain volume in cubic inches that determines how many wires of a certain size may be brought into it.

Electrical boxes for rewiring work come in many types and sizes. These boxes, sometimes called "old-work" or "cut-in" boxes, differ from many new-work boxes in that they mount easily where wall and ceiling coverings are already in place. Select a size large enough to hold all the necessary wires and the number of switches, receptacles, or combinations you want. For help in choosing sizes, consult Table IV on page 7.

WALL AND OUTLET BOXES

Electrical connections must be made in an electrical box that has a removable cover. Wall boxes are rectangular in shape and are used for switches and receptacles. Some metal wall boxes have removable sides and can be ganged together to form a box large enough to hold more than one device. Outlet boxes are usually octagonal or square. They are used to hold devices, mount fixtures, and protect wire connections. Table IV on page 7 shows the number of wires you may bring into any particular size box. For wiring in previously

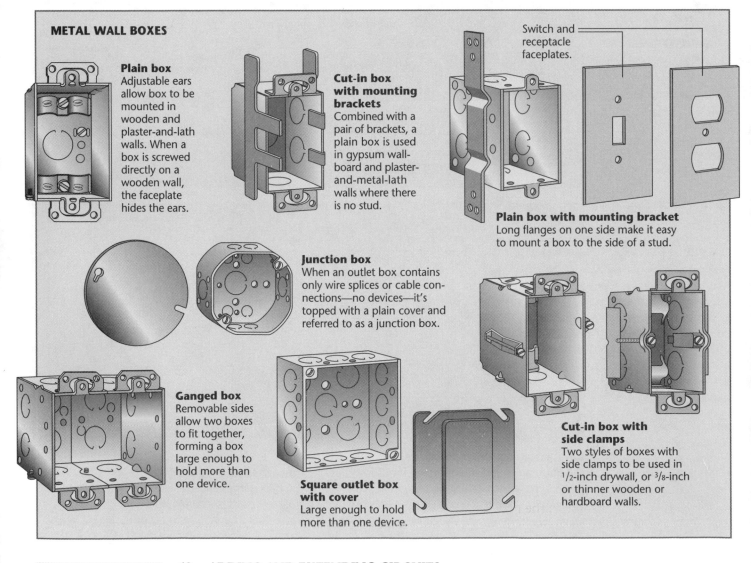

METAL WALL BOXES

Plain box
Adjustable ears allow box to be mounted in wooden and plaster-and-lath walls. When a box is screwed directly on a wooden wall, the faceplate hides the ears.

Cut-in box with mounting brackets
Combined with a pair of brackets, a plain box is used in gypsum wallboard and plaster-and-metal-lath walls where there is no stud.

Switch and receptacle faceplates.

Plain box with mounting bracket
Long flanges on one side make it easy to mount a box to the side of a stud.

Junction box
When an outlet box contains only wire splices or cable connections—no devices—it's topped with a plain cover and referred to as a junction box.

Ganged box
Removable sides allow two boxes to fit together, forming a box large enough to hold more than one device.

Square outlet box with cover
Large enough to hold more than one device.

Cut-in box with side clamps
Two styles of boxes with side clamps to be used in 1/2-inch drywall, or 3/8-inch or thinner wooden or hardboard walls.

covered walls, you'll be choosing between cut-in boxes and plain boxes with adjustable top and bottom ears. The right type depends on the wall it goes into. Several typical styles are shown opposite and at right.

CEILING BOXES

Beyond merely providing a place for joining wires and connecting them to a device, a ceiling box often supports a heavy fixture. Because of this, a ceiling box is usually fastened to a joist by a flange attached to the box or by an adjustable or an offset hanger bar.

For hanging a lightweight fixture (24 ounces or less) or a fixture with a canopy lip of 1/4 inch or more, consider a ceiling cut-in box or a pancake box. Different types of ceiling boxes are shown on page 70.

WHERE TO LOCATE BOXES

Keep all box heights consistent. If you're putting new ones in a room that already has boxes, consider putting the new boxes at the same height as the old ones. Place new receptacle boxes 12 to 18 inches above the floor. New switch boxes are best installed 44 to 48 inches high. The location of light fixtures is up to you—be sure they'll shed light efficiently where needed. All boxes must be accessible—even junction boxes that contain no devices. They must not be covered by walls, ceilings, or floors. After you've located a stud and marked the holes, the next step is to cut them. For a tidy cut in gypsum wallboard, use a saber saw or a keyhole saw.

Every box—whether it's a switch, receptacle, or junction box—must be accessible. Except in kitchens, don't put boxes for receptacles too low or too high. Avoid putting a switch box behind a door or on the hinge side. In new construction, put either the top or the bottom of a switch box 48 inches from the floor.

Knockouts: Cable enters metal boxes through prestamped knockout openings. To remove one, use a screwdriver and a hammer to strike the knockout, then twist off the punched-out knockout with slip-joint pliers. If you are working with nonmetallic boxes, use a screwdriver to punch in the knockout.

Mounting arrangements: Whether a box is metal or nonmetallic, there are four main mounting methods: internal screw, external nail or bracket, hanger bar, and grippers. The illustrations at right and on pages 68 and 70 show boxes with these mounting arrangements. There are about as many kinds of external brackets as there are situations in which boxes are mounted. Before you buy a box, consider where you're going to mount it. You can save a lot of time by getting a box with brackets to suit your needs. If you want to hang an outlet box between two joists but don't have a box with a hangar bar, you can nail a 2x4 between the joists and attach the box directly to the wood. Mount your boxes so that they will be flush with the finished wall surface.

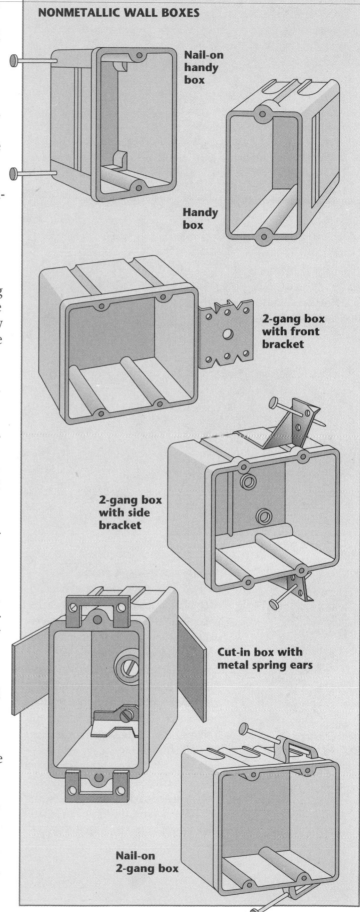

NONMETALLIC WALL BOXES

Nail-on handy box

Handy box

2-gang box with front bracket

2-gang box with side bracket

Cut-in box with metal spring ears

Nail-on 2-gang box

CEILING BOXES

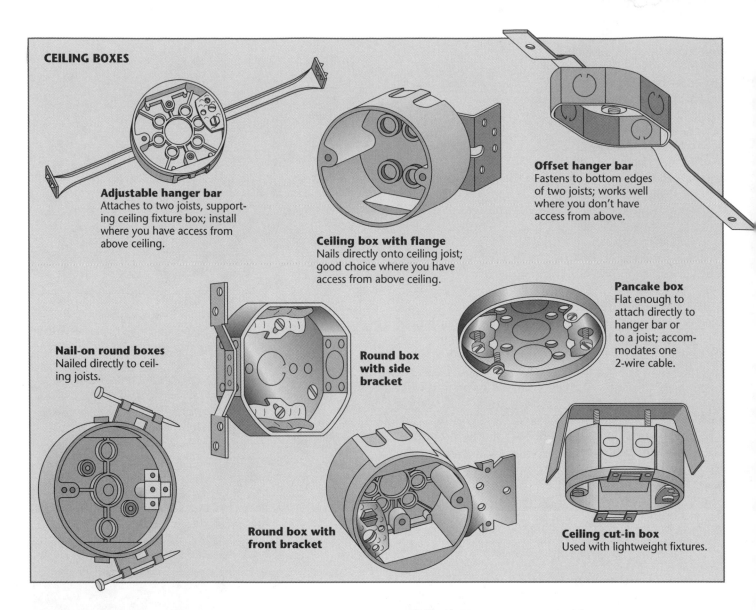

Adjustable hanger bar
Attaches to two joists, supporting ceiling fixture box; install where you have access from above ceiling.

Ceiling box with flange
Nails directly onto ceiling joist; good choice where you have access from above ceiling.

Offset hanger bar
Fastens to bottom edges of two joists; works well where you don't have access from above.

Nail-on round boxes
Nailed directly to ceiling joists.

Round box with side bracket

Pancake box
Flat enough to attach directly to hanger bar or to a joist; accommodates one 2-wire cable.

Round box with front bracket

Ceiling cut-in box
Used with lightweight fixtures.

Preparing to install a wall box

TOOLKIT

For gypsum wallboard or wood:
• Keyhole or saber saw

For plaster:
• Cold chisel
• Utility knife
• Keyhole or saber saw
• Diagonal-cutting pliers (optional)

1 ▶ Locating a stud
To install a box in an existing wall, plan to install the box between two studs. The surest, most accurate way to find a suitable location for the box without cutting into the wall is to drill a small test hole where you want the box. Bend an 8" to 9" length of stiff wire slightly, push it through the hole, and revolve it (*right*). If it bumps into a stud or a fire block, move over a few inches and try again until you find an empty space. When locating a box on a plaster-and-wood-lath wall, chip away enough plaster around the test hole to expose a full width of lath. Plan to center the box on the lath.

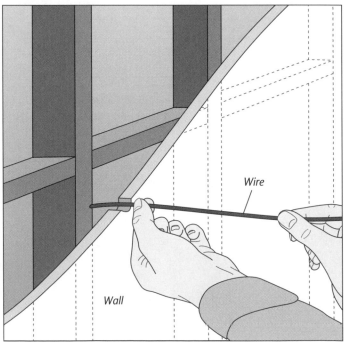

Wire

Wall

2 ▶ Marking the wall box hole

Once you've found a clear space, you can mark the wall or ceiling for cutting the box hole. For a plain wall-mounted box, place box face down on a sheet of thick paper or cardboard to be used as a template. Trace the box's outline, omitting the adjustable top and bottom ears. For cut-in boxes with side clamps, trace around the side clamps. Cut the template out in the shape of the box and position it on the wall at the chosen location, traced side facing the wall. Scribe the outline on the wall *(right)*.

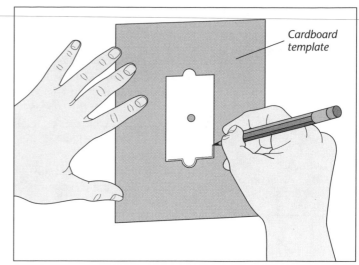

Cardboard template

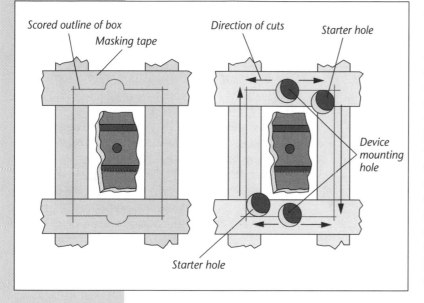

Scored outline of box

Masking tape

Direction of cuts

Starter hole

Device mounting hole

Starter hole

3 ◀ Cutting holes in the wall

For a tidy cut in gypsum wallboard or wood, use a saber saw or a keyhole saw. Though cutting away large areas of plaster-and-wood-lath isn't recommended because of the difficulty of patching up, cutting small holes for boxes is possible. Use a cold chisel to chip away enough plaster to expose one width of lath. To prevent excess plaster from cracking, tape the outside border of the hole outline with wide masking tape. Score the outline several times with a utility knife. Then drill holes as shown at left for starting a keyhole or saber saw blade and turning corners. Cut slowly and evenly in the direction of the arrows (lath is usually extremely tough and fibrous; it's difficult to cut). Once you've cleared the opening, remove the tape. When cutting a ceiling hole, brace the ceiling as you cut so large chunks of plaster don't break away.

CUTTING HOLES IN PLASTER-AND-METAL-LATH AND WOOD

Plaster-and-metal-lath. Trace the box outline on the wall and then tape the border with wide masking tape to prevent excess plaster from cracking. Use a metal bit to drill starter holes, then chisel away plaster within the box outline. Cut out the metal lath with a metal-cutting blade on a saber saw or mini-hacksaw, or use a pair of diagonal-cutting pliers.

Wood. Clean cuts are easy to make in wood. Trace the box outline on the wall, drill starter holes, and then cut with a keyhole or saber saw.

🔲 ASK A PRO

WHAT'S THE BEST WAY TO LOCATE A STUD IF THE WALL COVERING IS ALREADY INSTALLED?

Hunting for studs can be an uncertain job. Sometimes you can measure to find them on 16-inch centers, but not always. You can knock on the wall with your knuckles, listening for a solid rap that indicates something behind the wall covering, but knocks often sound alike all over the wall. An electronic stud finder, shown at right, is a very effective way to locate studs. These small gadgets have a magnetic pointer that is attracted to nail heads, but they work only on walls covered with gypsum wallboard or on wooden walls.

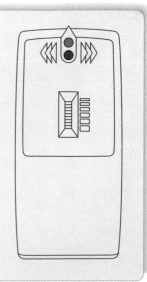

Mounting wall boxes

TOOLKIT
- Keyhole or saber saw
- Cable ripper
- Wire stripper
- Drill and bit
- Screwdriver
- Slip-joint pliers (for installation in gypsum wallboard)

Installing a box in a plaster-and-wood lath wall

Screw a cable connector to the box (or use a box with integral clamps that make fitting the box in the hole easier). Check the box for proper fit in the hole. If necessary, adjust the ears so the front edge of the box is flush with the finished wall surface. Next, mark screw placements on the lath at the top and bottom of the hole. Remove the box and drill pilot holes for screws, then screw the box to the lath *(right)*. (On wooden walls, just screw the ears to the wall surface; the faceplate will hide the ears and screws.)

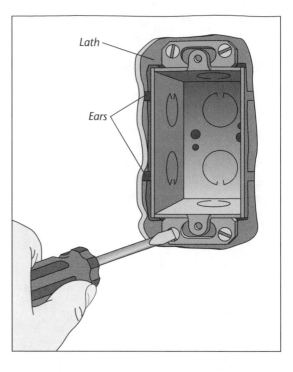

Lath

Ears

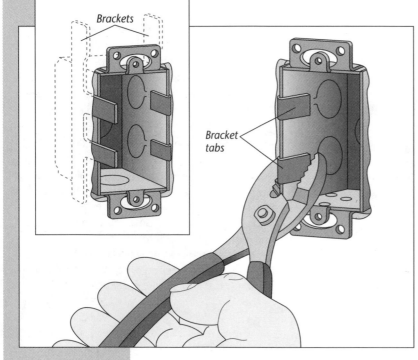

Brackets

Bracket tabs

Installing a box in gypsum wallboard

Test fit the box in the hole. Screw a cable connector to the box (or use a box with integral clamps that make fitting the box in the hole easier). If necessary, adjust the ears so the front edge of the box will be flush with the finished wall. Put the two brackets in the wall, one on either side of the box, and pull the bracket tabs toward you so they're snug against the backside of the wall *(inset)*. Then bend the tabs over the sides of the box and secure them with slip-joint pliers *(left)*.

Installing a cut-in box

Screw a cable connector to the box (or use a box with integral clamps that make fitting the box in the hole easier) and thread the cable through. Leave 6" to 8" of cable sticking out of the box for connections. Mounting this box is a one-time proposition. Once inside the wall or ceiling, the side teeth flare away from the box, making it difficult to remove. Tightening the screw at the back of the box simply pushes the teeth into the back side of the wall surface *(right)*. Because you can't remove the box, be sure the cables are in place and the box fits the hole before you mount the box. (To try out fit, remove metal spring ears from box.)

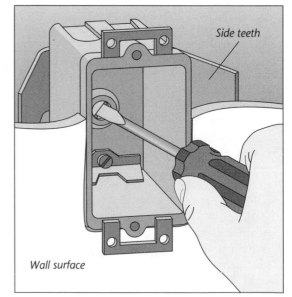

Side teeth

Wall surface

TOOLKIT
• Drill and bit
• Tools to remove attic flooring
• Keyhole or saber saw
• Cable ripper
• Wire stripper
• Screwdriver or hammer

Preparing to install a ceiling box

A cut-in box for gypsum wallboard fits into a simple hole—just hold the box against the wall and mark around its perimeter. For a ceiling box, if you have access above from an attic, mark the hole from above. To do this, first locate the box from below and drill a small guide hole through the ceiling. If your attic has a floor, you'll need a long extension bit for drilling up through the flooring (in this case the guide hole must be considerably larger). Next, remove any attic flooring at that spot and outline the box on the back side of the ceiling *(right)*.

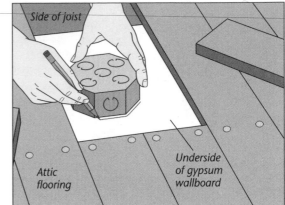

Side of joist

Attic flooring

Underside of gypsum wallboard

Installing a ceiling box with offset hanger

Screw a cable connector to the box (or use a box with integral clamps that makes fitting the box in the hole easier) and thread the cable through. Leave 6" to 8" of cable sticking out of the box for connections. Remove 4" of outer sheathing and prepare the wire ends *(page 11)*. This box works well where you don't have access from above. Screw the offset hanger bar to the bottom edges of two joists *(right)*. If you don't have access from an attic, you must cut out the ceiling material between two joists. Screw the hanger bar to the bottom edges of the joists.

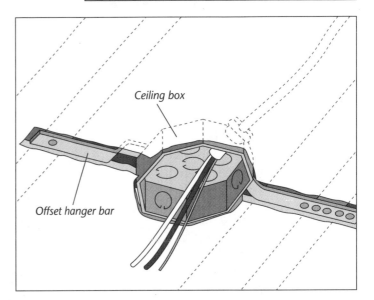

Ceiling box

Offset hanger bar

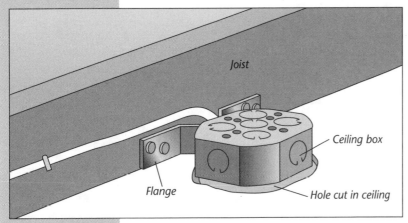

Joist

Ceiling box

Flange

Hole cut in ceiling

Installing a ceiling box with flange

Screw a cable connector to the box (or use a box with integral clamps that makes fitting the box in the hole easier) and thread the cable through. Leave 6" to 8" of cable sticking out of the box for connections. Remove 4" of outer sheathing and prepare the wire ends *(page 11)*. If you don't have access from above, you'll have to cut out a rectangle from the ceiling material. Nail or screw the flange to a joist *(left)*.

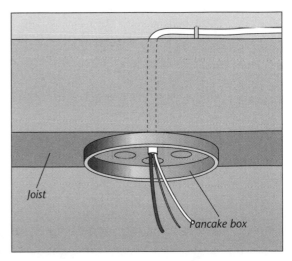

Joist

Pancake box

Installing a pancake box

Screw a cable connector to the box (or use a box with integral clamps) and thread the cable through. Leave 6" to 8" of cable sticking out of the box for connections. Remove 4" of outer sheathing and prepare the wire ends *(page 11)*. Simply screw this box to a joist or beam, as shown at right. Position the box so it will hide the hole that was drilled for the cable. Do not make cable junctions in this kind of box.

Using a built-in cable clamp

Cable must be secured to electrical boxes using built-in cable clamps or external cable connectors *(right)*. To connect cable to a box with a built-in clamp, you may have to remove the clamp screw and cable clamp to pry out a knockout located behind the clamp. Feed the cable into the box through a knockout, leaving 6" to 8" extending into the box for wire connections. Tighten the built-in clamp so that it holds the cable securely but does not bite into the sheathing. Loosen the grounding screw at the back of the box, hook the grounding wire around the screw clockwise and tighten the screw to secure the connection.

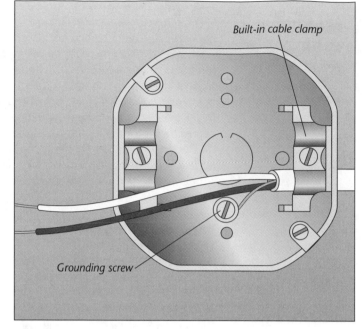

Built-in cable clamp

Grounding screw

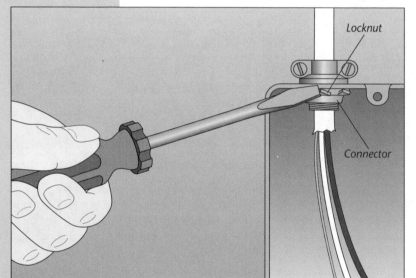

Locknut

Connector

Installing a metal cable connector

Pry out a knockout in the box. Unscrew the locknut on the connector, then pull the cable through the connector, allowing 6" to 8" of cable to make the wire connections. Tighten the screws on the cable connector, then push the connector through the knockout in the box. Slide on the locknut and use a screwdriver to tighten it securely *(left)*.

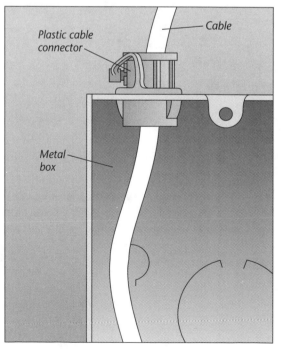

Plastic cable connector

Cable

Metal box

Installing a plastic cable connector

Pry out a knockout in the box. Firmly push the connector into the knockout hole, then pull the cable through the connector, allowing 6" to 8" of cable to make the wire connections. To secure the connector, insert the plastic wedge in the slot. A plastic connector is difficult to remove once it is installed.

Grounding within boxes

TOOLKIT
• Screwdriver
• Multipurpose tool (optional)

Using a grounding clip

As with most other terminal connectors, a grounding screw or a grounding clip is equipped to receive only one wire. To ground a switch, self-grounding receptacle, or light fixture in a metal box that is the last box of a circuit run, hook the grounding wire around the grounding screw at the back of the box, or use a grounding clip to attach it to the side of box *(right)*.

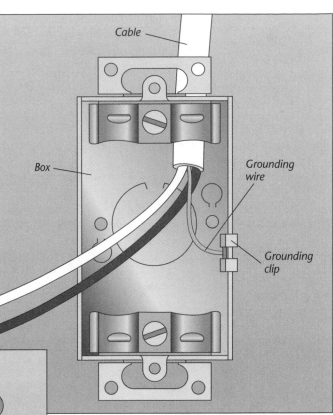

Cable

Box

Grounding wire

Grounding clip

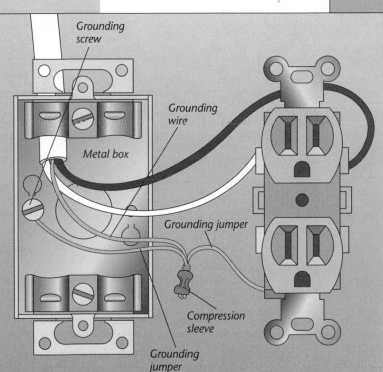

Grounding screw

Grounding wire

Metal box

Grounding jumper

Compression sleeve

Grounding jumper

Using a grounding jumper

To ground a switch, self-grounding receptacle, or a light fixture that is in a metal box that is not the last box of a circuit run, you must use a grounding jumper. For the grounding jumper, use wire that is the same size as the circuit wires. Secure one grounding jumper to the grounding screw at the back of the box, and secure another grounding jumper to the grounding screw on the receptacle *(left)*. Twist all grounding wires and jumpers together and crimp them with a compression sleeve or use a wire nut to secure the connection *(page 12)*.

📐 ASK A PRO

HOW DO I CONNECT CABLE TO A NONMETALLIC BOX?

Cable knockouts in nonmetallic boxes are held in place with thin webs of plastic. Break out a knockout wherever NM cable will enter a box. NM cable need not be clamped to a nonmetallic box if it is stapled within 8 inches of the box. In old work, where you're fishing cable behind walls, ceilings, and floors, you may not be able to support a cable within 8 inches of a box. In this case, you must clamp the cable to the box.

TOOLKIT
• Screwdriver
• Neon tester (for wiring into a switch)

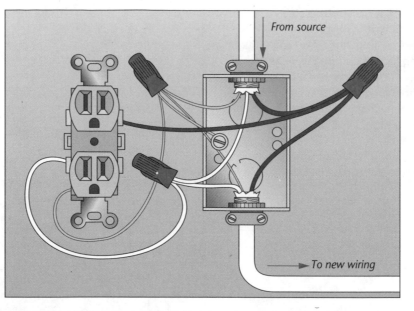

From source

To new wiring

How to wire into a receptacle
De-energize the circuit *(page 21)* and gently pull the receptacle from the box. Secure the white wires from the cables together with a white jumper wire attached to a silver screw terminal and screw on a wire nut. Repeat the procedure for the black wires, attaching the jumper to a brass screw terminal. Secure the new grounding wire together with the other grounding wires and a jumper wire to the box.

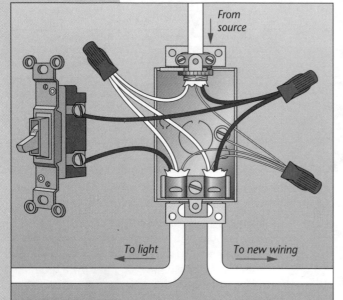

From source

To light

To new wiring

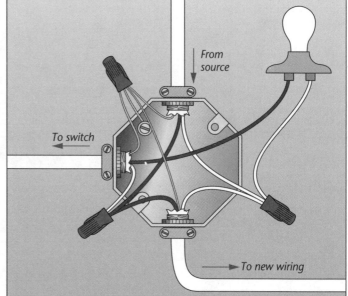

From source

To switch

To new wiring

How to wire into a switch
Pull the switch from the box and use a neon tester to locate the hot black wire *(page 8)*. Turn off power to the circuit. Follow the procedure for wiring into a receptacle, taking care to secure the black wire from the new cable to the hot wire.

How to wire into a fixture
Pull the fixture from the box and confirm that the power is off *(page 8)*. Connect the wires in the new cable as shown above.

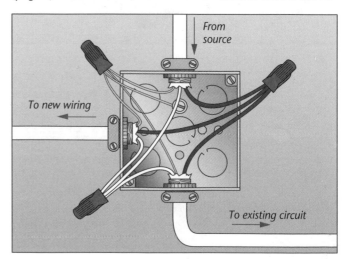

From source

To new wiring

To existing circuit

How to wire into a junction box
Remove the cover from the junction box and confirm that the power is off *(page 8)*. The illustration at right shows a typical wiring extension from an existing junction box.

Finishing up

TOOLKIT
- Wide-blade putty knife
- Trowel

Patching up the holes

When the holes are cut and the cable is routed from the source to the new box locations, the only remaining jobs are mounting the boxes, making the wiring connections, and doing the patch-up work. If you've notched into walls or ceilings in the process of wiring, now is the time to make them look like new. Here are some tips for putting everything back together. In plaster walls and ceilings, the *National Electrical Code* requires that you repair plaster around boxes so there are no gaps or open spaces at the edge of the box. Patching around a box is a simple matter. Use a wide-blade putty knife to apply commercial plaster compound (*right*). Try to match the texture of the surrounding wall. For larger holes you'll have to provide some backing (such as lath), clean and moisten the edges of the hole, and, in some cases, apply more than one coat.

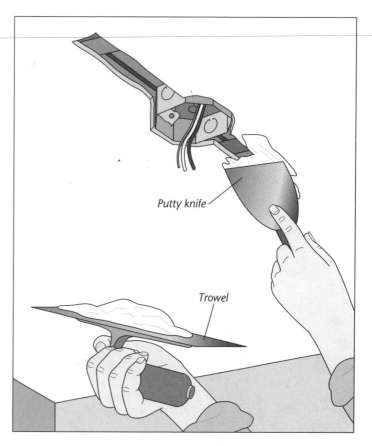

Putty knife

Trowel

MAKING REPAIRS TO GYPSUM WALLBOARD

For small repairs, just use a wide-blade putty knife and some spackling compound.

To replace a larger section, you'll need to cut a new piece of wallboard to fill the hole. If there are no structural members on which to nail the replacement piece, add some wooden blocks for support.

Nail up the replacement piece, dimpling the surface slightly at the nail heads. Use a wide-blade putty knife to spread joint compound across the dimples. With joint tape and compound, cover the edge joints around the replacement. Spread a layer of compound over the tape, being careful not to let the putty knife dip into the joint. Let the compound dry.

Apply a second coat of compound to the nail heads and tape, feathering the edges of the first coat to produce a relatively smooth surface. Sand nail dimples and joints when dry.

For a smooth wall, you may have to apply a third coat to both joints and nail heads and sand again.

To duplicate a skip-trowel texture, apply a large amount of joint compound with a broad palette knife and draw the blade over the surface in one direction. A plaster texture is applied with the same tool, moving it in a semicircular motion. Duplicate a stipple finish with a paintbrush.

Let dry, then paint the surface.

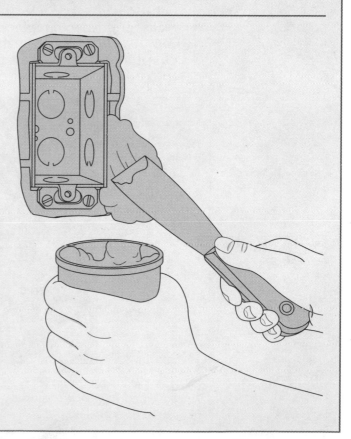

TELEPHONE WIRING

Since the advent of modular telephone plugs in the mid-1960s, installing a new telephone has been as simple as plugging in a lamp. But where? Many, if not most, homes are inadequately wired to meet today's communication needs. Until recently, new homes were built with only one or two telephone jacks; one in the kitchen, usually, and perhaps an extension jack in the master bedroom. But as the chart on page 80 shows, today's standards have dramatically changed.

The good news is that upgrading your home telephone wiring is remarkably simple. A wide selection of do-it-yourself products is designed for fast home installation. With these modular components, everything plugs into everything else. A screwdriver and a Saturday afternoon may be all you need to upgrade or completely rewire your home's telephone system.

This chapter will acquaint you with the basics of home telephone wiring—how to route exposed telephone wiring, as well as wiring that is concealed behind walls. You'll learn how to install new modular jacks, and how to replace older outlets. Adapted from *The Telephone Book* * available from AT&T Corp., this chapter also shows how to use a telephone line tester to confirm that everything is working properly.

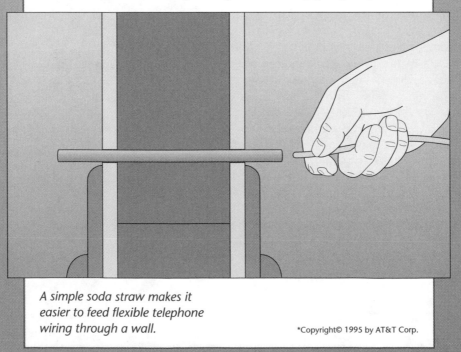

A simple soda straw makes it easier to feed flexible telephone wiring through a wall.

HOME TELEPHONE WIRING RECOMMENDATIONS

It's easy to modify and improve your home telephone system. You can replace old-style rotary telephones, add new phones and accessories, even rewire your entire home to accommodate computers, home security, or energy management systems. The illustration below shows an updated home telephone system that uses modular equipment. Use it as a guide when install-ing a new telephone system, or when upgrading your existing system.

Although telephone lines conduct low-voltage elec-trical current that is unlikely to cause any harm, you should observe some safety precautions. Never work on an active line; first disconnect the wiring at the inter-face jack, or take a telephone handset off the hook.

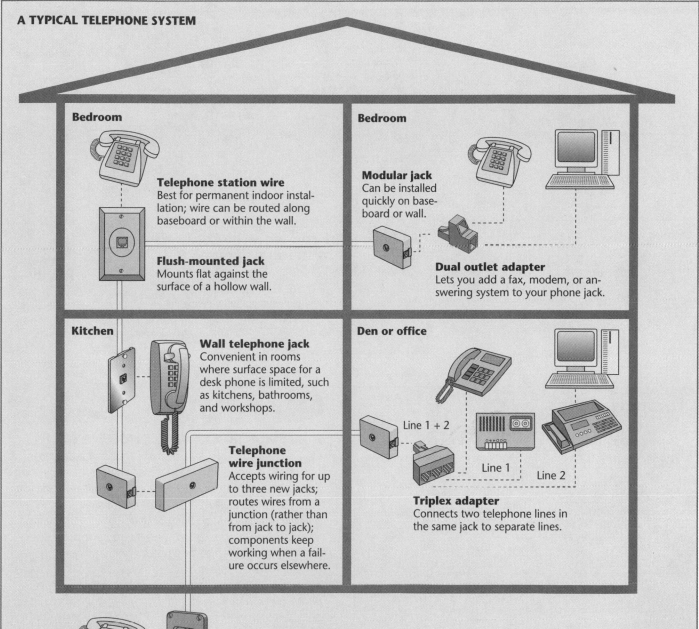

A TYPICAL TELEPHONE SYSTEM

Bedroom

Telephone station wire
Best for permanent indoor instal-lation; wire can be routed along baseboard or within the wall.

Flush-mounted jack
Mounts flat against the surface of a hollow wall.

Bedroom

Modular jack
Can be installed quickly on base-board or wall.

Dual outlet adapter
Lets you add a fax, modem, or an-swering system to your phone jack.

Kitchen

Wall telephone jack
Convenient in rooms where surface space for a desk phone is limited, such as kitchens, bathrooms, and workshops.

Telephone wire junction
Accepts wiring for up to three new jacks; routes wires from a junction (rather than from jack to jack); components keep working when a fail-ure occurs elsewhere.

Den or office

Line 1 + 2

Line 1

Line 2

Triplex adapter
Connects two telephone lines in the same jack to separate lines.

Outdoor modular jack
Weatherproof jack ideal for porches, patios, and balconies; hinged cap seals out moisture and dust when jack is not in use.

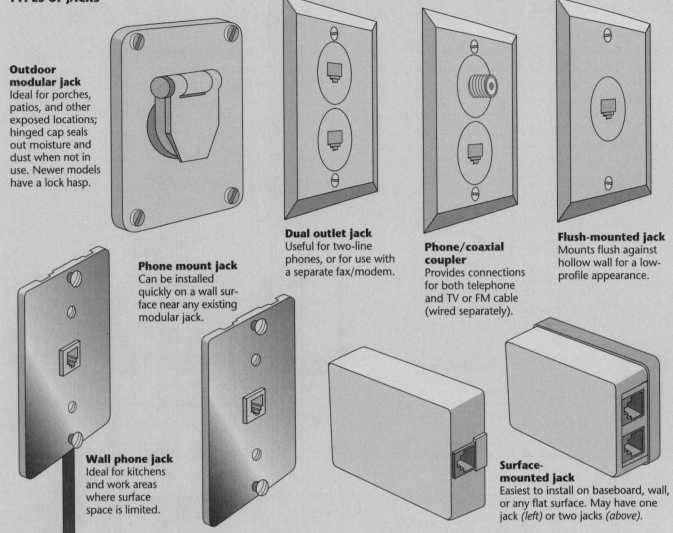

TYPES OF JACKS

Outdoor modular jack
Ideal for porches, patios, and other exposed locations; hinged cap seals out moisture and dust when not in use. Newer models have a lock hasp.

Phone mount jack
Can be installed quickly on a wall surface near any existing modular jack.

Dual outlet jack
Useful for two-line phones, or for use with a separate fax/modem.

Phone/coaxial coupler
Provides connections for both telephone and TV or FM cable (wired separately).

Flush-mounted jack
Mounts flush against hollow wall for a low-profile appearance.

Wall phone jack
Ideal for kitchens and work areas where surface space is limited.

Surface-mounted jack
Easiest to install on baseboard, wall, or any flat surface. May have one jack (*left*) or two jacks (*above*).

RECOMMENDED JACKS

Living room	Phone/coaxial coupler
Dining room	Single outlet phone jack
Master bedroom	Phone/coaxial coupler
Child's room	Dual outlet phone jack
Guest bedroom	Flush-mounted jack
Den/family room	Phone/coaxial coupler
Home office	Dual outlet phone jack
Kitchen	Wall phone jack
Utility room	Wall phone jack
Garage	Wall phone jack
Patio/balcony	Outdoor modular jack

ASK A PRO

HOW MANY JACKS DOES MY HOME NEED?

Only a few years ago, one or two telephone jacks may have been adequate for most homes. But not today—due to the popularity of products and services that depend on telephone links to the outside world. Home fax machines and answering systems have become commonplace. More advanced applications include home security systems, computer e-mail, and a rich variety of new services accessible by computer modem. To satisfy this increasing need, many builders now routinely install 15 to 20 telephone jacks in new homes. If your telephone system does not meet your demands, consider expanding your telephone wiring—both for your own convenience, and to add value to your home. A general rule of thumb: Plan to install at least one jack per room; two in all key living spaces, or any room larger than 150 square feet.

INSTALLING TELEPHONE WIRING

When installing a telephone wiring system, remember that jacks should be installed no farther than 200 feet from the point where wiring first enters your home. Before you begin any installation work, sketch a floor plan of your home showing where each jack will be installed. Try to choose the straightest and most direct wire routes.

Avoid installing wire in damp locations, or in places where the telephone wire may come into contact with hot surfaces such as steam pipes, heating ducts, and hot water pipes.

Protect wiring from abrasion and possible damage. Do not route wire where it may be crimped or broken, such as through window or door openings. Never route loose or unprotected wire across stairwells, door openings, carpet walkways, or other open spaces where it could present a tripping hazard. For a safer and more attractive installation, route wiring along the top surface of baseboards, the bottom surface of wainscoting and chair rails, beneath carpet edges, or in other protected locations.

Provide adequate support for wiring. Use fasteners that do not puncture or abrade wire insulation, and space them closely enough to support the wire securely.

Isolate telephone wire from electrical wiring and other possible sources of interference. Try to keep telephone wiring well away from electrical outlets. Never install telephone wires in a conduit or junction box with electrical wiring. If you must route telephone wiring across or parallel to any other kind of wiring, follow the guidelines listed in the chart at right.

After installing any new jacks or wiring, conduct the tests described on page 88 to make sure everything has been connected correctly. When in doubt, contact your telephone company or an electrical contractor for advice.

MINIMUM WIRE SEPARATION	
Bare electric light wiring, or electric power wire of any kind (wire with no insulation)	5'
Single-conductor insulated wire (not more than 300 volts)	2"
Wire in conduit, in armored or nonmetallic sheath cable, or power-ground wires	None
Radio or television antenna lead-in or ground wires	4 "
Signal or control wires	None
Cable TV wiring (coaxial cable with grounded shielding)	None
Telephone drop wire (wire entering house from telephone pole or junction box) —if protector is fused —if not fused, or if no protector	2"* None
Neon signs or any wiring associated with a transformer	6"
Lightning rods or wires	6'**

* If minimum separation cannot be maintained, enclose wiring in a plastic tube, wire guard, or two layers of vinyl tape extending 2" beyond the point where telephone wiring crosses the other wire.

** Less than 6' of separation is acceptable if telephone, power, and lightning-rod grounds are all connected to a common metallic, cold-water pipe that is properly grounded; or if separately driven ground rods are used for telephone, power, and lightning rods, and the rods are bonded together.

TYPES OF WIRING PLANS

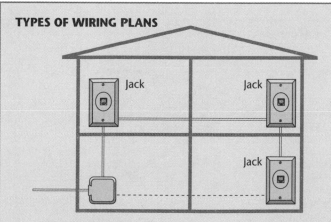

Loop wiring
Adequate for homes smaller than 3,000 square feet, or homes with modest requirements. From the point where wiring enters the home, a single telephone wire runs from jack to jack. For added protection, run an extra wire from the last jack back to the starting point (dotted line). If the wire is damaged, telephone service to other rooms is maintained.

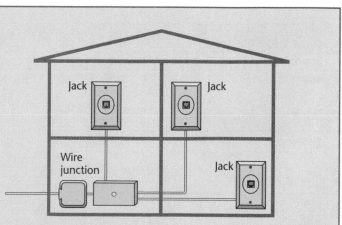

Home run wiring
Each jack is connected to a wire junction at the point where wiring enters the home. Telephone lines can be added or changed without rewiring; damaged wires can be repaired without disturbing the rest of the service in other rooms of the home.

WIRES AND CORDS

Modern modular telephone systems employ three basic types of wire, shown below. Handset cords are used only to connect the handset to the telephone. They cannot be used to connect a phone to a jack; they are not wired in the same way as line cords, and their modular plugs are a different size. Some telephones (usually models with the dial in the handset) require special handset cords; be sure to check carefully when replacing a handset cord.

Line cord: Line cord is flat, four-conductor cord that plugs into a jack to connect a telephone or other accessory (such as a fax or modem). Never splice line cords to create a longer cord; use a small adapter that allows you to plug two cords together. If you want to place a tele-

phone more than 25 feet from an existing jack, it's better to run more permanent station wire to a new jack.

Telephone station wire: Designed for most home telephone wiring, station wire is intended for permanent indoor installation and should never be used outdoors without special protection, such as conduit. Station wire can contain four, six, or eight conductors, each sheathed in color-coded insulation. Always maintain the continuity of the color coding throughout all the wiring in your home. Connect red to red, green to green, etc. However, some types of wire—especially in older homes—may use a different color scheme. If you must mix wire types, use the chart below as a guide.

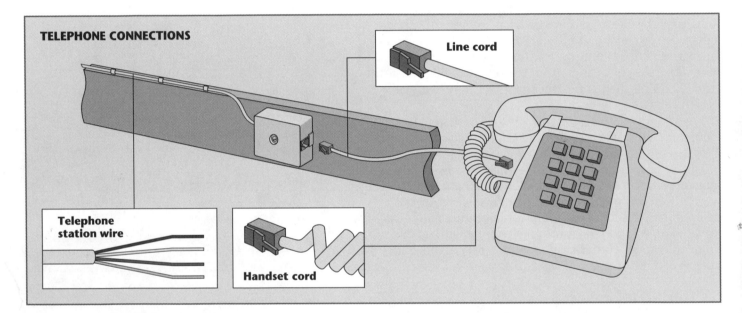

TELEPHONE CONNECTIONS

Line cord

Telephone station wire

Handset cord

WIRE COLOR CODING

Standard 2-pair wire	Alternate types
Red	Blue (white bands) Blue
Green	White (blue bands)
Yellow	Orange (white bands) Orange
Black	White (orange bands)
Standard 3-pair wire	
Red	Blue (white bands)
Green	White (blue bands)
Yellow	Orange (white bands)
Black	White (orange bands)
Blue	Green (white bands)
White	White (green bands)

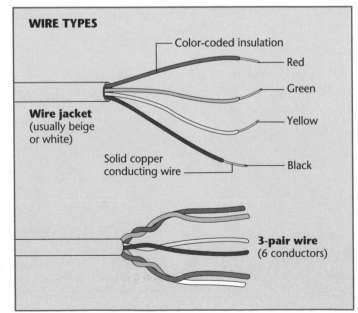

WIRE TYPES

Color-coded insulation

Red

Green

Yellow

Wire jacket (usually beige or white)

Solid copper conducting wire

Black

3-pair wire (6 conductors)

EXTENDING A CIRCUIT

Choose a route where the wire will be inconspicuous and well protected. Run it inside cabinets and closets, or beneath shelving if possible. In paneled rooms, wire can be concealed under panels, hollow corner trim, and baseboard molding. It also can be routed along baseboards, door and window frames, picture molding, or chair rails. Make sure to secure the cable well.

Wire can be concealed beneath carpeting where the carpet meets the wall. If the carpet edges are tacked down, remove tacks with pliers or a screwdriver tip, or use pliers to lift up a tack strip.

Route wire around a door frame rather than running it across a doorway on the floor. If you must run the wire on the floor, protect the wire by covering it with a metal door sill or carpet sealing strip. Use clips to hold the wiring in place.

Floor-to-floor wiring can be routed inside hollow walls. To run wire down from the ceiling, the wall must be hollow from top to bottom. Sound the wall by tapping to find a location between studs with no cross-bracing to block the wire path. Avoid walls containing electrical wires. Interior walls are more suitable for routing wire.

Installing exposed wiring

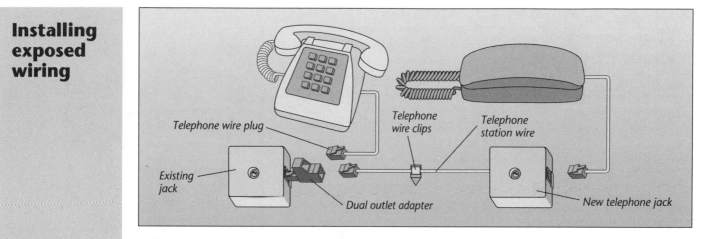

Telephone wire plug

Telephone wire clips

Telephone station wire

Existing jack

Dual outlet adapter

New telephone jack

Routing wiring along baseboards

A recommended route is to run wire along the top of baseboards and use telephone wire clips to secure it. Use your thumb or the tip of a screwdriver handle to press the clips behind the baseboard. Wire clips also include an adhesive pad that can be used to fasten wire to most smooth surfaces. Whichever method you use, space clips at intervals no greater than 16". Round corners by bending the wire in a gentle curve, and install a clip on each wall 2" from the corner.

Installing concealed wiring

TOOLKIT
• Drill and 1/4" bit

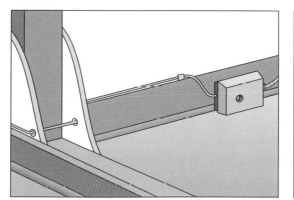

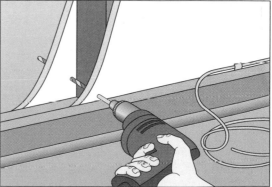

1 Routing wire through walls

Drilling through a wall is often the easiest way to route wire into another room. In homes with typical gypsum wallboard walls, this is usually a simple job. First, find a suitable location for the wire extension; a typical extension is shown above left. To avoid drilling through wall studs, knock on the wall until you hear a hollow sound. Then, use a drill with a 1/4" bit (at least 5" long) to drill through the gypsum wallboard, just above the baseboard (*above, right*).

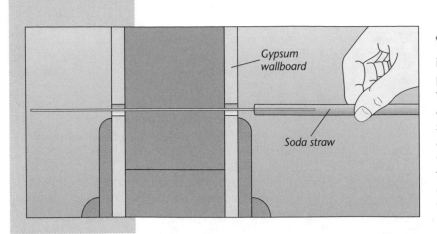

Gypsum wallboard

Soda straw

2 **Feeding the wire**
Since telephone wire is limp and difficult to insert through holes in both sides of a hollow wall, push a soda straw through first, then insert the wire through the straw. If you still have difficulty, push a length of coat hanger wire through the wall first, slip the straw over it, then remove the coat hanger and push the telephone wire through the straw. Once the wire is through, remove the straw. For a finished appearance, holes can be sealed with putty or a quick-setting plaster, and painted over after the wire has been installed.

Routing wire from floor to floor

TOOLKIT
• Drill with extra-long bit

Making the holes and fishing the wire

Using a drill with a long bit, drill diagonally through the floor to the top plate of the wall below *(right, above)*. If routing wire down from a ceiling, use an extra-long drill bit ($1/4$" to $3/8$" diameter) to drill a hole through the top plate of the wall. Drill another hole through the wall just above the baseboard, directly beneath the first hole. Fasten a weight to a strong string and drop the string down the inside of the wall to the floor. Use a length of stiff coat hanger wire bent into a hook to snare the string and pull it out through the lower hole. If you have difficulty snaring the string, have someone in the attic move the string around until it is in a better position. Tie the string to the telephone wire and wrap the knot with tape to prevent it from being snagged inside the wall. Working from the attic, pull the string through the lower hole and up through the wall until the wire emerges in the attic. Use a similar procedure to route wire up from a basement or crawl space. Lower the weighted string from a hole drilled above the baseboard and use the coat hanger to snare it from the basement, through a hole drilled in the bottom plate of the wall *(right, below)*.

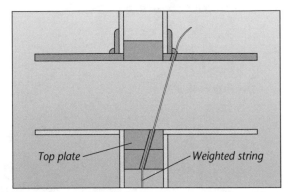

Top plate   Weighted string

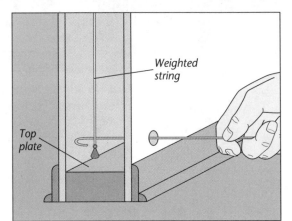

Weighted string

Top plate

ASK A PRO

HOW SHOULD I DRILL INTO A WALL?

When drilling through a wall, be careful to avoid hidden pipes, ducts, or wiring. Never drill near an electrical outlet. Determine wall thickness and composition before drilling. Gypsum wallboard walls are usually $4^1/2$ inches thick, but in older homes may be thicker. Use a fluted or spade bit for wood and wallboard walls and a carbide bit for masonry walls (right). Drill just above the baseboard, at least five inches from any door or window openings. Sound the wall by tapping to locate studs and cross-braces. Tap the wall lightly with a screwdriver handle wrapped in clean cloth, and drill where the wall sounds hollow.

Fluted bit

Carbide-tipped bit

Bit extension and spade bit

Installing new modular jacks

TOOLKIT
- Telephone line tester
- Screwdriver
- Keyhole or saber saw

Installing a surface-mounted jack
Remove 2" of wire jacket from the source wire *(page 89)*. Loosen the terminal screws on the front of the base. Insert the red wire into the slot marked "red" on the back of the base until 1/4" of wire emerges. Repeat the procedure for each wire, matching it with the color-coded slots. Match the colored wires from the jack cover with the terminals on the front of the base. Slide the appropriate spade tip under each screw head and tighten the terminal screws. Screw on the cover.

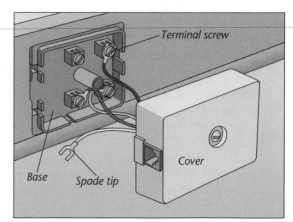

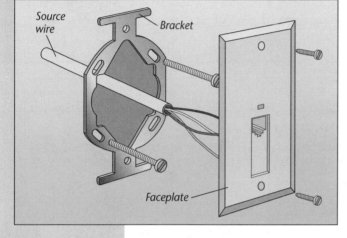

Installing a flush-mounted jack
Install flush-mounted jacks between wall studs where there is no electrical wiring, mounting them at the same height as receptacles. To install a jack, position the bracket on the wall and trace its outline. Use a saw to cut away wall material within the circular outline. Screw the mounting bracket to the wall, aligning it with the hole. Remove 3" of outer jacket from the source wire *(page 89)*. Loosen the four terminal screws located on the back of the faceplate. Insert each color-coded wire into the appropriate slot on the faceplate until it contacts the plastic barrier. Bend the wire ends upward and tighten the terminal screws. Screw the faceplate to the bracket.

Installing a modular jack
Screw the backplate to the wall and remove 3" of wire jacket from the source wire *(page 89)*. Fit the yellow wire into the slot on the far right side of the connector cap, extending the wire 1/4". Bend it down until it fits into the grooves. Repeat the procedure with the other wires. Fold back the clear plastic flaps to expose the backplate connectors. Matching wire colors, slip the cap onto the bottom of a connector. Repeat the procedure with the other connector cap, then screw on the faceplate.

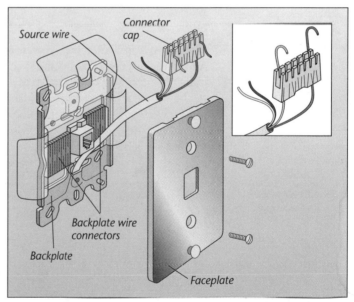

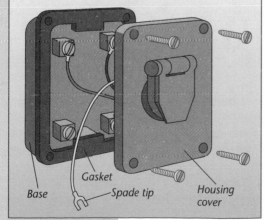

Installing an outdoor jack
Using screws or anchor bolts, mount the base of the jack housing so that the grommet hole is at the bottom; make sure that the jack is at least 16" above the ground. From inside the housing base, push the grommet into the grommet hole until the grommet is firmly seated. Measure and cut telephone wire, stripping about 5" of wire jacket *(page 89)*. Hold the wires together and insert them into the grommet. Pull them through the grommet until about 1/4" of wire jacket is inside the box. Loosen the four screw terminals and insert each color-coded wire into the appropriate screw. Press the gasket in place on the housing base. Place the spade tips inside the housing cover under the appropriate terminal screw and tighten the screws. Attach the housing cover to the base.

1. Plan jack locations carefully before you begin. Look for convenient, easily accessible places where jacks will be protected, well away from electrical outlets. Remember that jacks should be installed no farther than 200 feet from the point where telephone wiring first enters your home.

2. Always read the installation instructions provided with each jack, and make sure all color-coded wires are attached to the correct terminal. Better quality jacks contain special terminals that can accommodate extra wire, to create a path to a new jack. Never insert more than one conductor into each slot of a terminal.

3. Never install jacks in locations that would permit someone to use a telephone near water. Typical locations for this are near a bathtub, laundry tub, wash bowl, kitchen sink, swimming pool, or in wet areas such as a damp basement.

4. Jacks installed in a kitchen should be located a reasonable distance from grounded surfaces such as sinks, refrigerators, and ranges.

5. After installing any new jack, conduct the tests described on page 88 to make sure it has been connected correctly.

Replacing older outlets

TOOLKIT
- Telephone line tester
- Screwdriver
- Keyhole or saber saw

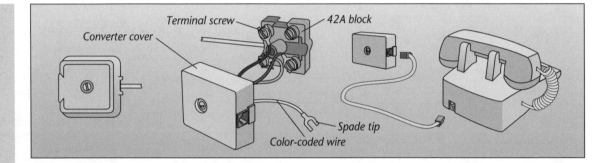

Installing a modular jack converter

A modular jack converter upgrades an old-style permanent telephone outlet, known as a 42A block, to the modular jack system. To install a modular jack converter, first remove the plastic cover of the 42A block and discard it. Next, inspect the connecting block base for cords that do not bring service into the connecting block or lead to other jacks. Gently bend these unused cords and wires away from the rest of the wires in the 42A block. Loosen the terminal screws and pull out the spade tips. Then, attach the converter wires to the proper terminal screws on the modular jack, respecting color coding, then attach the converter cover to the connecting block base.

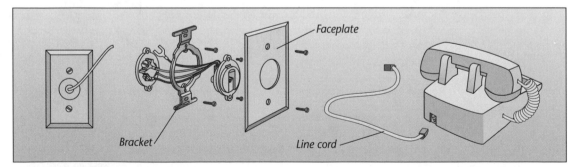

Installing a flush jack converter

A flush-mounted connection has a round or rectangular faceplate covering a junction box. A line cord runs from the telephone through a hole in the center of the faceplate. Install flush-mounted jacks between wall studs, mounting them at the same height as receptacles. Position the bracket on the wall, trace its outline, and use a saw to cut out wall material within the scored outline. Screw the mounting bracket to the wall, aligning it with the hole. Remove 3" of wire jacket from the end of the telephone wire *(page 89)*. Loosen the four terminal screws located on the back of the faceplate. Insert each color-coded wire into the appropriate slot on the faceplate until it touches the plastic barrier. Bend the wire ends and tighten the terminal screws, then screw the faceplate to the bracket.

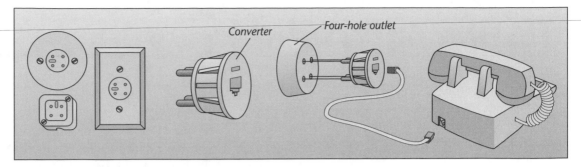

Converter   Four-hole outlet

Installing a plug-in converter

A type of outlet previously used for portable extension telephones, this kind of jack may be mounted on a wall or baseboard, or flush mounted in a junction box covered by a plastic faceplate. To install the four-prong jack, simply plug the converter into a four-hole outlet (round or square), then plug in your modular telephone. The converter can be removed. (Newer models are square, not round.)

Replacing older wall phones

TOOLKIT
- Screwdriver
- Diagonal-cutting pliers

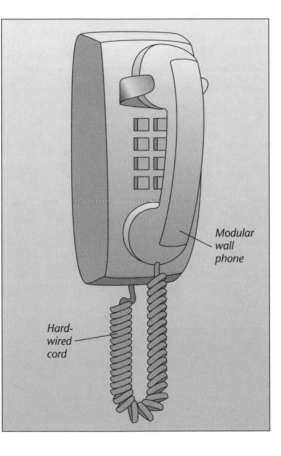

Modular wall phone

Hard-wired cord

1 ▶ Removing the telephone
Replacing most wall phones is simply a matter of lifting off the old one and plugging in the new one. If the old phone can't be unplugged, however, the task is more complex. Old, hard-wired wall phones can't be converted; you'll have to remove the telephone and install a new modular jack. First, remove the telephone housing. Most older wall phones have a small U-shaped hole where the coiled handset enters the phone. Inside this hole is a tab. To remove the housing, use the eraser end of a pencil to push the tab up while pressing the bottom of the phone toward the wall with your other hand. The housing should pop free easily. Wall phones that don't have these U-shaped holes are attached with screws, usually concealed beneath the telephone number card. To expose these screws, use a bent paper clip to remove the clear plastic cover, then lift out the number card.

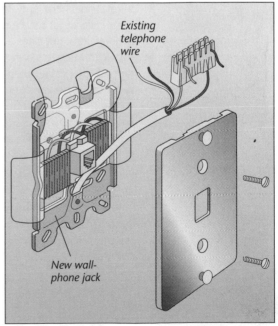

Existing telephone wire

New wall-phone jack

2 ▶ Detaching the wires
After the housing is removed, remove the screws securing the telephone base to the wall and lift off the phone, exposing the wires (usually red, green, yellow, and black). These can simply be cut to remove the old phone, but be careful not to let the loose wires fall down inside the wall—you'll need them to connect a new modular jack. To prevent this, tie a string around an object nearby and tie the other end to one of the wires before you begin cutting. If the wire falls down into the wall after the last wire is cut, you can use the string to retrieve it. Install a modular jack (page 85).

TESTING AND TROUBLESHOOTING

After making any modifications to your telephone wiring, you should conduct a simple test to make sure everything is working properly. The most reliable way to check your wiring installation is by using a telephone line tester. These are available in most hardware and home-supply stores that stock telephone wiring components. If you don't have a line tester, you can use a working telephone to check wiring integrity. First, make sure the telephone is working properly. Plug it into a working jack and dial a number. (Use the first jack where telephone wiring enters your home if you can.) If the phone is not working properly, you can't use it for testing since a problem exists either in the telephone or in the telephone company wiring.

Perform the following tests at newly installed jacks, or any jack that may not be working properly.

Dial tone test: Plug the telephone into the jack, lift the handset and listen for a dial tone. If you hear nothing, you have a bad contact or a wrong connection. Open the jack and check to make sure all wires are connected firmly to wire terminals.

Tip/ring polarity test: If you hear a dial tone, dial a telephone number. If you continue to hear a dial tone during and after dialing, the red and green wires are reversed. Open the jack and switch the red and green wire connections. If you have two telephone lines and the same problem occurs on the second line, the yellow and black wires should be reversed.

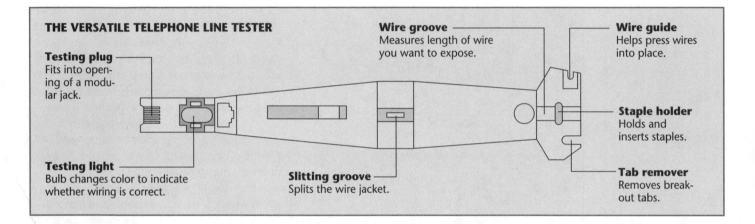

THE VERSATILE TELEPHONE LINE TESTER

Testing plug Fits into opening of a modular jack.

Wire groove Measures length of wire you want to expose.

Wire guide Helps press wires into place.

Testing light Bulb changes color to indicate whether wiring is correct.

Slitting groove Splits the wire jacket.

Staple holder Holds and inserts staples.

Tab remover Removes break-out tabs.

Using a line tester

TOOLKIT
• Hammer (for inserting staples)

Testing the red/green circuit
This test verifies the integrity of the red and green wire connections, the circuit that carries basic telephone service, or service for line 1 in a two-line home. A green light indicates that the wiring is correct. A red light indicates that the wires are reversed. To correct the problem, open the jack and reverse the red and green wire connections, then test again. If the tester does not light, open the jack and check to make sure the red and green wires are connected securely to the wire terminals.

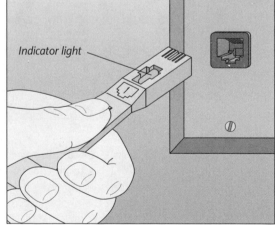

Indicator light

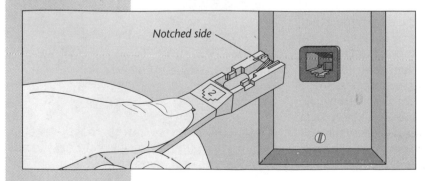

Notched side

Testing the yellow-black circuit
This test verifies the integrity of the yellow and black wire connections. This circuit may not be needed if you have only one line, but should be checked; it could be useful later to add another line, or to provide an alternate path for basic telephone service if the red/green circuit is damaged.

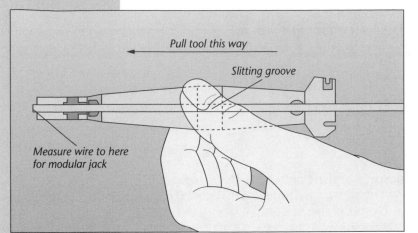

Pull tool this way

Slitting groove

Measure wire to here
for modular jack

Removing telephone wire jacket

Decide how much wire length you want to expose. If you want 3" required by a modular jack, line up the end of the telephone wire jacket with the bulb end of the telephone line tester *(left)*. Lead the wire jacket back over the slitting groove and press the wire into the groove with your thumb. With one hand, grip the wire leading off the staple holder end of the tool. With the other hand, move the tool toward the end of the wire, slitting the wire jacket. Peel out the color-coded wires from inside the wire jacket, and use scissors to cut off the wire jacket.

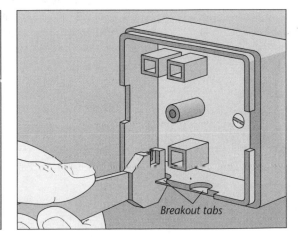

Inserting wire staples

Place a staple in the slot located in the end of the telephone line tester. Place the groove on the underside of the tool onto the telephone wire. Using a hammer, tap the staple into the mounting surface. Remove the tester and finish hammering, taking care not to puncture the wire *(left)*.

Telephone wire

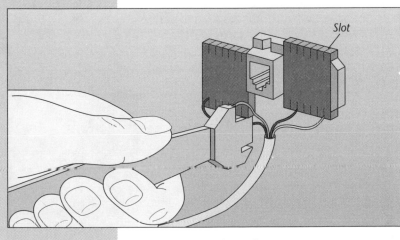

Slot

Breakout tabs

Guiding wires into slots

The telephone line tester equipped with a wire slitter also has a wire guide that ensures accurate placement of wires that must be inserted into slots. First place the wire into its appropriate slot with your finger. Then use the tool's wire guide to press the wire snugly into its slot *(above)*.

Removing a breakout tab

Breakout tabs are found along the edges of modular jacks and wire junctions and, when removed, provide a passageway for telephone wire. To remove a tab, fit the tab remover slot onto the selected breakout tab *(above)*. Using the tool, bend the tab back and forth until you can remove it.

OUTDOOR WIRING

Though the principles are the same for both indoor and outdoor wiring, some of the materials used in outdoor wiring projects are specially designed to resist the weather.

There are driptight subpanel boxes and watertight switch boxes that are able to withstand temporary immersion in water. Underground electrical cable has a thick solid plastic covering that makes it watertight when buried directly in the ground. Typically, however, cable is routed through rigid metallic and rigid non-metallic conduit, which protects it from the weather and from accidental damage from digging.

There are several ways to bring electricity outdoors. You can extend an inside power source by tapping into an existing switch, lighting, or receptacle outlet box, as shown in the illustrations on pages 93 and 94.

Temporary low-voltage lighting *(page 94)* is a safe and practical option for garden and patio lighting. Operating on only 12-volts, low-voltage wiring is easy to install and doesn't present the dangers of 120 volts.

When working with electricity outdoors, be extra careful. Always de-energize the circuit before working on it—even to change a light bulb. Make sure that outdoor circuits are grounded; run a copper grounding conductor the same size as the circuit conductors from source to load. For extra safety, use ground fault circuit interrupters (GFCIs) on all outdoor circuits.

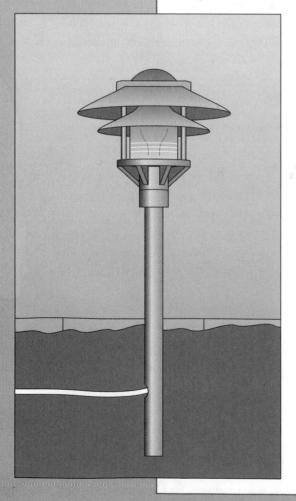

Easy to install and safe to operate, a few strategically placed low-voltage fixtures shed accent lighting on patios and other areas of your backyard.

MATERIALS MAKE THE DIFFERENCE

Electrically, there is no difference between wiring inside and outside—it's the materials that make the difference. Because outdoor wiring must survive the elements, materials are stronger and more corrosion resistant. Also, everything must fit exactly, so heavy-duty gaskets are often used to seal boxes, thus preventing water from entering them. Shown below are many of the devices that you will need for outdoor wiring projects.

BOXES
Outdoor fixtures come in two types: so-called "driptight" fixtures that seal against vertically falling water and "watertight" ones that seal against water coming from any direction. It is important to know which type you need and which type you have purchased.

Driptight: Usually made of sheet metal and then painted, driptight fixtures often have shrouds or shields that deflect rain falling from above. A typical driptight subpanel is shown below. This unit is not waterproof and must be mounted where floods, or even "rain" from sprinklers below, cannot touch it.

Watertight: Fixtures designed to withstand temporary immersion or sprinkling are watertight. Made of cast aluminum, zinc-dipped iron, or bronze, these fixtures have threaded entries. All covers for watertight boxes are sealed with gaskets; many of them are equipped with an exterior lever that enables you to operate the switch without opening the cover. The watertight switch box, shown below, is a typical outdoor box.

GROUND FAULT CIRCUIT INTERRUPTERS
According to present electrical codes, any new outside receptacle (such as one used to plug in a patio charcoal starter, or to plug in a radio) must be protected with a GFCI *(page 49)*. To make your job easier when you are tapping into an existing circuit, you can buy a complete kit consisting of a cast aluminum box and cover and a GFCI receptacle.

CONDUIT
Designed to enclose and protect outdoor wiring, conduit shields conductors from moisture and physical harm. Conduit is sized according to its inside diameter, coming in sizes ranging from ½ inch to 6 inches. The size you need depends on the number and size of conductors the conduit will be holding. In order of preference for the homeowner, conduits for underground use are rigid nonmetallic and rigid metal. Rigid nonmetallic (PVC schedule 40) requires a separate grounding wire. It must be buried at least 18 inches deep unless it is cov-

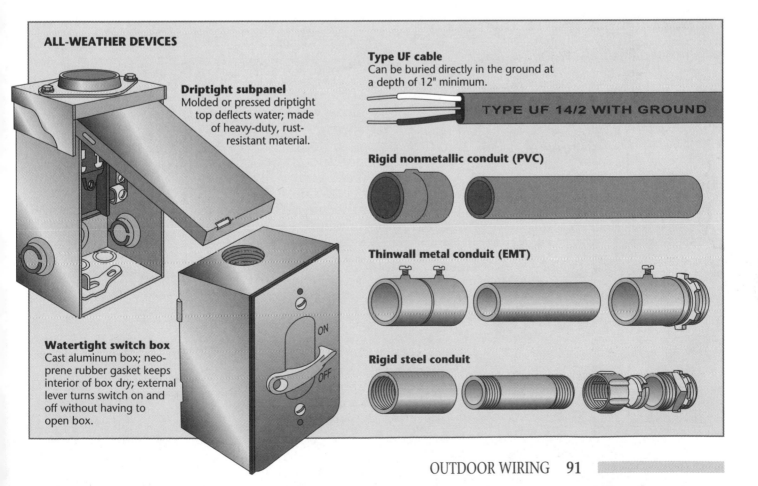

ALL-WEATHER DEVICES

Driptight subpanel
Molded or pressed driptight top deflects water; made of heavy-duty, rust-resistant material.

Watertight switch box
Cast aluminum box; neoprene rubber gasket keeps interior of box dry; external lever turns switch on and off without having to open box.

Type UF cable
Can be buried directly in the ground at a depth of 12" minimum.

TYPE UF 14/2 WITH GROUND

Rigid nonmetallic conduit (PVC)

Thinwall metal conduit (EMT)

Rigid steel conduit

ered with a concrete cap; in that case it can be buried at a lesser depth. One advantage of rigid nonmetallic conduit is that it does not corrode.

Rigid metal conduit will corrode and eventually disintegrate in certain types of soils. One advantage of this type of conduit is that it may be directly buried only 6 or more inches deep. In addition, unless it's used to feed a swimming pool, it doesn't require a separate grounding wire.

Thinwall conduit (EMT) is not recommended for underground burial. Used with watertight couplings and connectors, however, EMT is a good choice in exposed locations above ground level. You must use some type of conduit to protect the conductors wherever they are exposed to physical abuse; EMT is a good choice in these situations. The illustration below shows a typical outdoor installation; refer to it for ideas on how to plan your outdoor wiring projects.

ASK A PRO

CAN I BURY CABLE IN MY BACK YARD?
You can bury type UF cable (page 91) directly in the ground. However, there are some restrictions. The National Electrical Code permits burial of this cable only 12 inches deep for residential branch circuits if it is used for a 120- or 120/240-volt branch circuit. When burying UF cable, however, dig as deep as possible (12 inches minimum). Lay a redwood board on top of the cable before covering it with dirt (right). This reduces the danger of spading through the cable at a later time. Do not make the mistake of using NM cable underground.

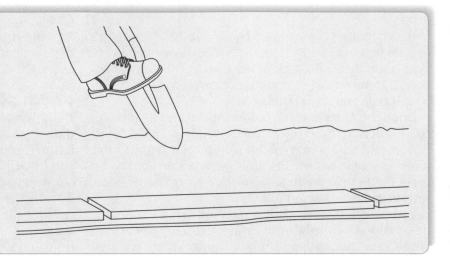

A TYPICAL OUTDOOR INSTALLATION

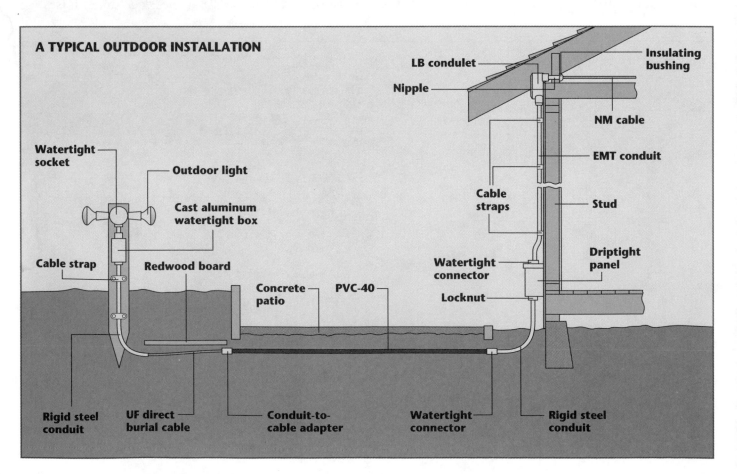

Outdoor power sources

Extending a cable to an outdoor device

Extending a circuit to the outside of your house requires the same procedures as extending a circuit indoors *(pages 54 to 77)*. You can tap into existing switch, lighting, and receptacle outlet boxes that are in the middle or at the end of a circuit run. The cable extension diagrams below show how to extend wiring from an attic or crawl space *(below, left)*, and from an existing porch light *(below, right)*. Refer to the diagrams for a list of materials you will need to make the circuit extension.

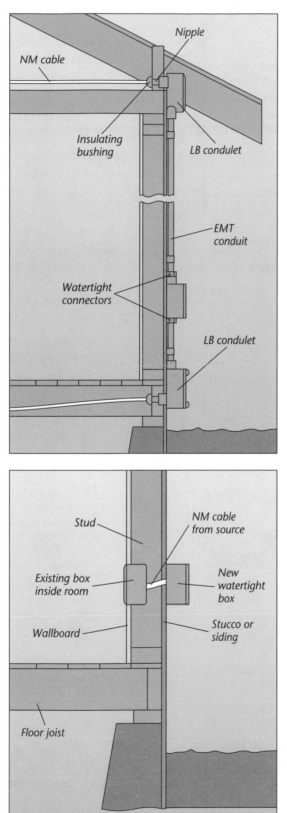

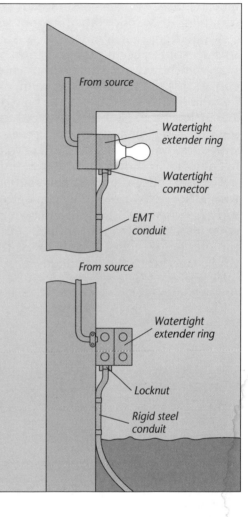

Extending a cable from an existing box inside the house

The cable extension diagram at left shows how to install a new watertight receptacle box back-to-back with an existing box in an interior room. In this example, a hole is drilled through the outside wall, and the cable is fed from the existing box to the new box location. NM cable can be used because the cable is not exposed to the weather. Refer to the diagram for a list of materials you will need to make the circuit extension.

LOW-VOLTAGE LIGHTING

Operating at only 12 volts, low-voltage wiring is easy to install and doesn't present the dangers of 120 volts.

A transformer, usually housed in a driptight, waterproof box, is used to step the 120 volts down to 12 volts. This much reduced voltage does not require the special conduit and boxes of other outdoor wiring.

A watertight switch or receptacle is a good choice for a power source. Mount the transformer near the power source and then run direct burial cable from the low-voltage side of the transformer to the desired locations for your lights. The cable can be buried in the ground a few inches deep. However, to avoid accidentally spading through it, consider running the cable alongside structures, walks, and fences where you won't be likely to cultivate, as shown in the illustration below.

The low-voltage lighting fixtures attach directly to the wiring. Some fixtures simply clip onto the wire; others must be wired into the system. Low-voltage lights also come in a kit with a transformer of the proper size for the number of lights. Be sure to use the exact size of wire called for in the instructions.

POOLS AND HOT TUBS

An above-ground pool or a hot tub usually is not permanently wired but is plugged into an outdoor receptacle. Any of these pools should be used only on a GFCI-protected circuit, even if your home was built before GFCIs were required. In addition, if the pool or tub is not already equipped with a twist-lock plug, it is recommended that you install one. Then wire a special GFCI-protected twist-lock receptacle so the pool is protected by a GFCI circuit. The illustration below shows a GFCI breaker installed in a subpanel; the pool's electrical devices are plugged into this protected circuit.

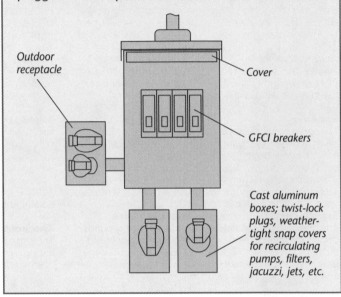

Outdoor receptacle

Cover

GFCI breakers

Cast aluminum boxes; twist-lock plugs, weathertight snap covers for recirculating pumps, filters, jacuzzi, jets, etc.

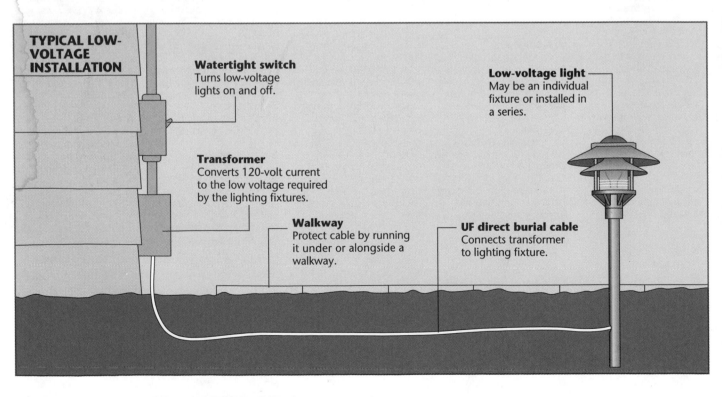

TYPICAL LOW-VOLTAGE INSTALLATION

Watertight switch
Turns low-voltage lights on and off.

Transformer
Converts 120-volt current to the low voltage required by the lighting fixtures.

Walkway
Protect cable by running it under or alongside a walkway.

Low-voltage light
May be an individual fixture or installed in a series.

UF direct burial cable
Connects transformer to lighting fixture.

WIRING GLOSSARY

Ampacity
Coined word combining ampere and capacity. Expresses in amperes the current-carrying capacity of electrical conductors.

Ampere
Unit used in measuring electrical current, based on the number of electrons flowing past a given point per second. Many elements of a wiring system are rated in amperes for the greatest amount of current they can safely carry. Abbreviated amp.

Armored cable
Flexible, metallic-clad cable (also known as BX cable) used for residential wiring.

Bonding
Connecting metal components of an electrical system to form a continuous conductive path capable of handling any current likely to flow.

Branch circuit
Any one of many separate circuits distributing electricity throughout a house from the last overcurrent device protecting the circuit.

Circuit
Two or more wires providing a path for electrical current to flow from the source through some device using electricity (such as a light) and back to the source.

Circuit breaker
Safety switch installed in circuit to break electricity flow automatically when current exceeds a predetermined amount.

Conductor
Technical term for electrical wire.

Conduit
A metal or PVC pipe that is designed to shield conductors from moisture and physical harm.

Current
Movement or flow of electrons through a conductor; measured in amperes.

Ground
Any conducting body, such as a metal cold-water pipe or a metal rod driven solidly into the earth, that provides electrical current with a path to the ground. Sometimes called "grounding electrode." Also, to connect any part of an electrical wiring system to the ground.

Grounding electrode conductor
Conductor that connects neutral bus bar of service panel to ground. Sometimes referred to as a "ground wire."

Grounding wire
Conductor that grounds a metal component but does not carry current during normal operation. Returns current to source in order to open circuit breaker or fuse if metal component accidentally becomes electrically alive.

Hot bus bars
Solid metal bars connected to main power source in service panel and subpanel. Branch circuit hot wires are connected to them.

Hot wire
Ungrounded conductor carrying electrical current forward from the source. Usually identified by black or red insulation, but may be any color other than white, gray, or green.

Insulation
Material that does not carry current, such as the color-coded thermoplastic insulation on wires.

Joist
Horizontal wooden framing member placed on edge, as in a floor or ceiling joist.

Jumper wire
Short piece of wire connected to the electrical box or to an electrical device, such as a switch or receptacle.

Kilowatt
Unit of electrical power equal to 1,000 watts. Abbreviated kw.

Kilowatt-hour
Unit used for metering and selling electricity. One kilowatt-hour equals 1,000 watts used for one hour (or any equivalent, such as 500 watts used for two hours). Abbreviated kwh.

Knockout
Prestamped circular impression in metal electrical boxes that is removed so that cable can enter the box.

Neutral bus bar
Solid metal bar in service panel or subpanel which provides a common terminal for all neutral wires. In service panel, neutral bus bar is bonded to metal cabinet and is in direct contact with earth through grounding electrode conductor. All neutral and grounding wires are connected to this bus bar. In subpanel, only neutral wires are connected to neutral bus bar, which "floats" in metal cabinet (it is not bonded).

Neutral wire
Grounded conductor that completes a circuit by providing a return path to the source. Except for a few switching situations, neutral wires must never be interrupted by a fuse, circuit breaker, or switch. Always identified by white or gray insulation.

Ohm
The unit of measurement for electrical resistance or impedance.

Overcurrent protection device
Fuse or circuit breaker that shuts off electricity flow when a conductor carries more than a predetermined amount of current.

Pigtail splice
When three or more wires are connected together, the connection is referred to as a pigtail splice.

Resistance
Property of an electric circuit that restricts the flow of current. Always measured in ohms.

Screw terminal
Threaded screw found on sockets, switches, and receptacles; used to make wire connections.

Service entrance conductors
Wires connecting terminals of service entrance equipment to either the service drop (if service is overhead) or the service lateral (underground service).

Service panel
Main power cabinet through which electricity enters a home wiring system. Contains main disconnect and grounding connection for entire system; sometimes called a fusebox, panel box, or service entrance panel.

Stud
Vertical wooden framing member; also referred to as a wall stud.

Type NM (nonmetallic) sheathed cable
A multiconductor, consisting of three or more wires that are contained within the same nonmetallic outer sheathing; used for interior wiring only.

Type UF (underground feeder) cable
A multiconductor, consisting of three or more wires that are contained within the same nonmetallic outer sheathing; used for exterior wiring only.

Underwriters' knot
Type of knot that relieves strain on the screw terminal connections on lamp sockets and some plugs.

Volt
Unit of measure denoting electrical pressure. Abbreviated V.

Voltage
Pressure at which a circuit operates, expressed in volts.

Watt
Unit of measurement for electrical power. One watt of power equals one volt of pressure times one ampere of current. Many electrical devices are rated in watts according to the power they consume. Abbreviated W.

Wire
Single electrical conductor, usually made of copper and wrapped in a nonconducting, color-coded insulation.

INDEX

A-B-C

AC metal-clad cable, 6, 66, 67
Aluminum wiring, 6, 7
   switches, 42
Amperage, 16
Appliances:
   cords, 31, 33
   plugs, 31-33
   special receptacles, 49
   wattages, 29
Attics:
   routing cable, 59
Baseboards, 62
Basements:
   routing cable, 59
Boxes, 68-69
   armored cable, 67
   back-to-back, 63
   cable connectors, 10
   conductors per box, 7
   driptight, 91
   grounding, 24-25, 75
   installation, 70-72
   watertight, 91
Boxes, metallic, 68
   grounding, 24, 75
Boxes, nonmetallic, 69, 75
   grounding, 24-25, 75
Cable, 6
   access, 57
   AC metal-clad cable, 6, 66, 67
   armored, 6, 66, 67
   attaching, 58
   between back-to-back boxes, 63
   burying, 92
   connecting to boxes, 74
   estimating require-ments, 66
   fishing, 60-61, 64-65, 66
   nonmetallic sheathed (NM) cable, 6, 66
   ripping, 10
   routing, 54, 57-58, 66
   routing around door-ways, 63
   routing behind base-boards, 62
   routing behind walls, 63, 64
   routing through ceil-ings, 58, 65
   surface wiring, 61
   UF cable, 91
   wiring into power source, 76
   see also Wires
Cartridge fuses, 19, 20, 21

Ceilings:
   boxes, 69, 70, 73-74
   routing cable, 58, 65
Circuit breakers, 14, 19, 20, 21
Circuits, 16
   disconnecting, 21
   doorbells, 40
   extending, 55, 60-65
   new, 55, 58-59
   parallel, 17
   receptacles, 49-50
   series, 17
   shutting off, 21
   simple, 17
   split-circuit recepta-cles, 41, 50, 52
   switch circuits, 43-48
   testing, 8-9, 26
Codes, 17
Compression sleeves, 11,12
Conductors, 6, 7, 16
Conduit, 91, 92
Connections, 10-12
Continuity testers, 4, 8, 9
Copper conductors, 6, 7
Cords, 31
   extension cords, 33
   stranded wire, 13
Current, 16

D-E-F

Dimmer switches, 42
Doorbells, 40
Drilling, 84
Duplex receptacles, 48
Edison base fuses, 19, 20, 21
Electrical boxes.
   see Boxes
Electrical load, 28-29
Electrical shock, 18, 23
Electricians, 17
Electricity, 16
Extension cords, 33
Fluorescent fixtures, 30, 36
   ballasts, 36, 38
   tube holders, 36, 39
   tubes, 37
Four-way switches, 42
Fuses, 14, 19, 20, 21

G-H-I-J

Ground fault circuit interrupters, 49, 56
   exterior, 91
Grounding, 23
   within boxes, 75
   metallic boxes, 24
   nonmetallic boxes, 24-25
   receptacles, 52
Hot wires, 8, 15

Insulation:
   removal from wire, 10, 11, 13
Jacks (telephones), 80, 85-86

K-L

Kitchens, 56
Lamps, 34
   cords, 13, 31
   rewiring, 35
   sockets, 30, 34-35
Laundry areas, 56
Lighting, 30, 56
   fixtures, adding, 64-65
   fixtures, grounding, 25
   low-voltage exterior, 90
   switches, 43-46, 64-65
   troubleshooting, 22
   see also Fluorescent fixtures; Lamps
Line testers, 88-89
Load, 28-29

M-N

Maps:
   wiring plans, 26-27
Meters, 15, 16
Moldings, 62
Neon testers, 4, 8-9
Neutral wires, 15
NM cable.
   see Nonmetallic sheathed (NM) cable
Nonmetallic sheathed (NM) cable, 6, 66

O-P-Q-R

Outdoor wiring, 90
   boxes, 91
   cables, 91, 92
   power sources, 93
Outlets.
   see Receptacles
Parallel wiring, 17
Path of least resistance, 16
Permits, 17
Pigtail splices, 12
Plugs, 30, 31
   octopus connectors, 33
   screw terminal, 32
   self-connecting, 31
   see also Receptacles
Power failure, 22
Receptacles, 41, 48, 49-50, 56
   adapters, 33
   back-wiring, 51
   duplex, 48
   ground fault circuit interrupters, 49
   grounding, 25, 52
   specialized, 49
   split-circuit, 41, 50, 52
   switch-controlled, 50

S-T

Safety precautions, 8, 18
   color coding, 42
   connections, 12
   electrical shock, 18, 23
   extension cords, 33
   main disconnect, 20
   outdoor wiring, 90
   receptacle adapters, 33
   short circuits, 22, 23
   telephone wires, 79
Screw terminal plugs, 32
Self-connecting plugs, 31
Series wiring, 17
Service panels, 14, 15, 19, 20, 26, 55
   main disconnect, 20
   subpanels, 55
Service ratings, 26
Short circuits, 22, 23
Single-pole switches, 42, 43-44, 45
Split-circuit receptacles, 41, 50, 52
Stranded wire, 13
Studs:
   locating, 71
Subpanels, 55
Surface wiring, 61
Switch-controlled receptacles, 50
Switches, 41, 42
   adding, 64-65
   grounding, 25
   installation, 47
   receptacle controls, 50
   single-pole, 42, 43-44, 45
   three-way, 42, 44, 46
Telephone systems, 78, 79
   circuit extensions, 83-84
   jacks, 80, 85-86
   replacing older out-lets, 86
   troubleshooting, 88-89
   wiring, 81
Terminal connections, 11
Three-way switches, 42, 44, 46
Tools, 4, 5
   continuity testers, 4, 8, 9
   neon testers, 4, 8-9
Type "S" fuses, 19, 20

U-V-W-X-Y-Z

UF cable.
   see Underground feeder (UF) cable
Underground feeder (UF) cable, 6, 91
Underwriters' knots, 35

Voltage, 15, 16
Walls:
   boxes, 68-69, 70-72
   routing cable, 58
   studs, 71
Wattage, 16
Wire nuts, 10-11, 12
Wires, 6, 7
   color coding, 6, 42
   connections, 10-12, 10-13
   cords, 31, 33
   distance from tele-phone wires, 81
   stranded, 13
   stripping, 10-11
   see also Cable; Telephone systems
Wiring plans:
   mapping, 26-27
   telephone systems, 81